Tracking the Narrow Gauge from
Chama to Durango

MIKE BUTLER

AMERICA THROUGH TIME®
ADDING COLOR TO AMERICAN HISTORY

America Through Time is an imprint of Fonthill Media LLC
www.through-time.com
office@through-time.com

Published by Arcadia Publishing by arrangement with Fonthill Media LLC
For all general information, please contact Arcadia Publishing:
Telephone: 843-853-2070
Fax: 843-853-0044
E-mail: sales@arcadiapublishing.com
For customer service and orders:
Toll-Free 1-888-313-2665

www.arcadiapublishing.com

First published 2022

Copyright © Mike Butler 2022

ISBN 978-1-63499-382-1

Typeset in 10pt on 13 pt Sabon
Printed and bound in England

Acknowledgments

A 1988 trip with the Rocky Mountain Railroad Club from Chama by car to Pagosa Junction and Durango was the genesis for this book. Though the rails of the Denver and Rio Grande narrow-gauge train had been removed for nearly twenty years at that time, we wanted to see where the train had traveled and view the remaining railroad structures. In 2021, I duplicated that trip, which resulted in this book.

Thanks go to so many wonderful folks who made our Durango journey possible over the years. My wife, Mary Jane, and I started a bookstore in Durango in 1977, and our son, Jason, was born there. Western author Louis L'Amour autographed his books in our store every summer and ensured the store's success. Durango historian and friend Duane Smith signed his book *Rocky Mountain Boomtown: A History of Durango* in our store in celebration of Durango's centennial in 1980. Author Doris Osterwald of Denver visited our store every spring and sold us hundreds of copies of her book *Cinders & Smoke: A Mile By Mile Guide for the Durango & Silverton Narrow Gauge Railroad*. She went on to write a guidebook for every tourist railroad in Colorado. John Dillavou was president of the Rocky Mountain Railroad Club in Denver during my years there and was my great friend and co-worker at the Denver Parks and Recreation Department. Thanks also go to Alan Sutton, publisher of Fonthill Media/America Through Time, for publishing my books, and Kena Longabaugh of America Through Time for her editorial assistance.

Most of the historic photographs in this book are from the collection of the Friends of the Cumbres & Toltec Scenic Railroad (attributed in the captions as "Friends"). Thanks to photo archivist Wes Pfarner of the Friends for once again helping me to assemble the photographs. Unattributed photographs were taken by the author.

While researching this book, I consulted many sources (see Bibliography). However, any errors in the text are strictly my own.

Contents

Introduction

General William Jackson Palmer, founder of the Denver and Rio Grande Railroad (D&RG), had a dream of building a narrow-gauge railroad from Denver to El Paso and on to Mexico City. His dream, however, was blocked at Española, New Mexico, 35 miles north of the capital city of Santa Fe. It was blocked by the so-called "Treaty of Boston" in 1880, an agreement between the D&RG and the Atchison, Topeka and Santa Fe Railroad (AT&SF). The two railroads had been fighting over a route through the Royal Gorge in Colorado which would allow access to the rich silver mines at Leadville. The terms of the treaty state:

> The AT&SF agreed to give up the Royal Gorge route. In exchange, the D&RG agreed not to build a line east of Pueblo [Colorado] that would have competed with the AT&SF transcontinental line, and the D&RG agreed not to build any further south than Española, New Mexico, for a period of ten years. Thus, when the [D&RG] line to Española was completed on December 31, 1880, the ... line ended there.[1]

When his dream of a rail line to Mexico City was crushed by the Treaty of Boston, General Palmer turned his attention westward to the newly developed silver mines at Silverton in southwestern Colorado. Having reached the southern Colorado town of Antonito in 1880, the D&RG started building west instead of farther south. This "San Juan Extension" (named for the mountain range it would cross) of the narrow-gauge railroad proceeded west from Antonito to Chama, New Mexico, and then northwest to Durango and Silverton, Colorado. Why did Palmer choose narrow gauge (3 feet between rails) instead of standard gauge (4 feet, 8.5 inches between rails)?

"He figured that this narrow gauge would allow his locomotives the ability to cover the steep grades and tortuous curves that would be encountered crossing the Rocky Mountains."[2] The narrow-gauge engines and cars, while offering advantages for mountain railroading, also had some disadvantages:

Because the original narrow-gauge engines and cars were smaller and lighter than standard gauge equipment, they could be operated safely on lighter rails ... than could standard gauge equipment. Most narrow-gauge equipment, being short, can operate around sharper curves than can standard gauge trains. Unfortunately, the light rail and sharp curves limit the speed of trains. Slow schedules and the expense of transferring freight to standard gauge cars brought about the demise of nearly all narrow-gauge railroads in the United States.[3]

Two segments of the D&RG's narrow-gauge line of the 1880s remain in operation today with tourist passenger trains: the Cumbres & Toltec Scenic Railroad (C&TS) between Antonito, Colorado, and Chama, New Mexico; and the Durango & Silverton Narrow Gauge Railroad between Durango and Silverton, Colorado. In between these two segments, 111 miles of rail ran from Chama to Durango. Abandoned in 1969, the rails were soon taken up, leaving behind bridges, water tanks, and roadbed, some of which can still be seen today. This book will take you on the journey of tracking those 111 miles and finding the remnants of the D&RG narrow gauge that still exist. Branch lines extended off this trackage into the forests north and south of the main line, to haul out timber cut to supply sawmills, which dotted the landscape. The general route of these branch lines can be tracked today, and we will explore them also. Finally, there was a branch line built from Durango to Farmington, New Mexico, in 1905, and we will also track that one.

A word about the railroad's name is helpful for clarification here:

As part of the boom and bust west, the Denver & Rio Grande as a corporate entity was born, died and reborn under a variety of names. These include Denver & Rio Grande Railway, 1870–1886; Denver & Rio Grande Railroad Company, 1886–1921; and Denver & Rio Grande Western Railroad 1921–1970 ... Denver & Rio Grande is used as the phrase common to all the various companies ... and will be used throughout this document. This is also abbreviated as "D&RG."[4]

We will follow this practice and refer to the railroad throughout this book as "D&RG."

Before continuing our journey tracking the line, it is necessary to take a moment to describe the types of steam locomotives used by the D&RG on the line, since captions on photographs used throughout the book often identify locomotive types:

Early in the life of the ... line, the D&RG used T-12 class engines built by the Baldwin Locomotive Works between 1883 and 1884. These were ten-wheeled locomotives in a configuration of 4-6-0. This meant that there were four small non-powered pilot wheels (two on each side) at the front of the locomotive, followed by six larger power-driven wheels (three on each side) in the middle of the locomotive with no small trailing wheels at the back of the locomotive. These locomotives were numbered in the 160s and 170s. This engine type and C-19 class 2-8-0 locomotives were used on the ... line until the early 1930s.[5]

Needing more powerful locomotives to help eliminate double-heading engines on steep grades, the D&RG purchased fifteen of the K-27 series 2-8-2 locomotives from Baldwin in 1903, numbering them from 450 to 464. In 1923, the D&RG purchased ten 2-8-2 K-28 class locomotives from the American Locomotive Company and numbered them 470 to 479.

In 1925, Baldwin built ten 2-8-2 locomotives of the K-36 class for the D&RG, numbered in the 480s:

> These were the last new narrow-gauge engines purchased by the Rio Grande and were part of the general upgrading and rebuilding of their narrow- gauge routes during the 1920s. They were specifically designed for Colorado narrow-gauge and were evolved from 50 years of mountain railroading experience. [For] the many years ... in service, the 480s ... prove[d] to be some of the most efficient, tough, and well-liked locomotives ever built.[6]

Finally, the K-37 class 2-8-2 locomotives were rebuilt engines created by the D&RG. "They were originally built in 1902 by Baldwin as standard-gauge 2-8-0s ... In 1928 and 1930, 10 of the ... engines were rebuilt into narrow-gauge 2-8-2s in the D&RG's Burnham Shops at Denver."[7] These engines were numbered in the 490s.

With that introduction to locomotive types, let's start tracking the narrow gauge from Chama to Durango.

1

Building the San Juan Extension from Chama to Durango

"Chama" seems like a strange name for a town. It is not a Spanish word, yet many of the settlers and railroad workers were of Hispanic origin. The river the town is located next to is also named Chama. The name seems to have come from a native Pueblo settlement farther south along the river, known as "Tsama." At any rate, when the D&RG arrived in Chama in December 1880, the town was no more than a few tents and shacks. That soon changed however, with the railroad's construction of a water tank, roundhouse, section house, and depot. The D&RG designated Chama as a division point. "The primary purpose of a division point is the maintenance and repair of steam locomotives."[1] The repairs occurred in the original six-stall wooden roundhouse, built in 1882. Chama also became a shipping point for sheep, cattle, and lumber, and the town grew correspondingly with stores, homes, saloons, and churches.

Officially, the D&RG's San Juan Extension ran from Alamosa to Antonito, Colorado, west to Chama, New Mexico, and then on to Durango and Silverton. This book will cover the 111 miles of the Extension from Chama to Durango as shown on the milepost table and map on page 12.

After descending from the dizzying heights of Cumbres Pass to Chama, the D&RG narrow-gauge railroad then continued west following the courses of the Navajo River, San Juan River, Piedra River, Pine River, Florida River, and finally the Animas River.

Anxious to participate in the riches of Silverton, the D&RG built its line cross drainage, down into each valley and up over the intervening hills. It was indeed a roller-coaster profile, abounding in sharp curves and steep pitches which hampered any sort of efficient operation.[2]

Mile Post	Place Name	Elevation	Siding Capacity	Today's Road #
		Chama To Durango		
344.12	Chama	7863	RR Yard	CO 17
349.20	Willow Creek	7742	17	US 64
354.01	Azotea	7733	32	US 64
354.45	Continental Divide	7733		US 64
359.56	Biggs	7537	19	US 64
363.47	Monero	7252	63	US 64
366.89	Amargo	7009	30	US 64
369.55	Lumberton	6856	25	US 64
373.33	Dulce	6779	29	US 64
377.66	Navajo	6588	23	J 9
386.73	Juanita, CO	6341	23	CR 551
390.36	Pagosa Juntion (Gato)	6271	75	CR 550
395.23	Carracas	6173	39	CR 550
403.63	Arboles	6139	45	CO 151
410.81	Allison	6222	16	CO 151/CR 329
414.34	Tiffany	6344	33	CR 321
418.86	La Boca	6177	28	CO 172
425.74	Ignacio	6437	62	CO 172
432.9	Oxford (Grommet)	6611	10	CO 172
437.29	Florida	6717	30	CR 222
441.59	Falfa (Alfalfa)	6924	11	CO 172/CR221
449.13	Carbon Junction	6425	27	US 160/550
451.52	Durango	6520	RR Yard	US 160/550
Milepost designations as of 1949				
Note- 1962 reconstruction around Navajo Lake added four miles				

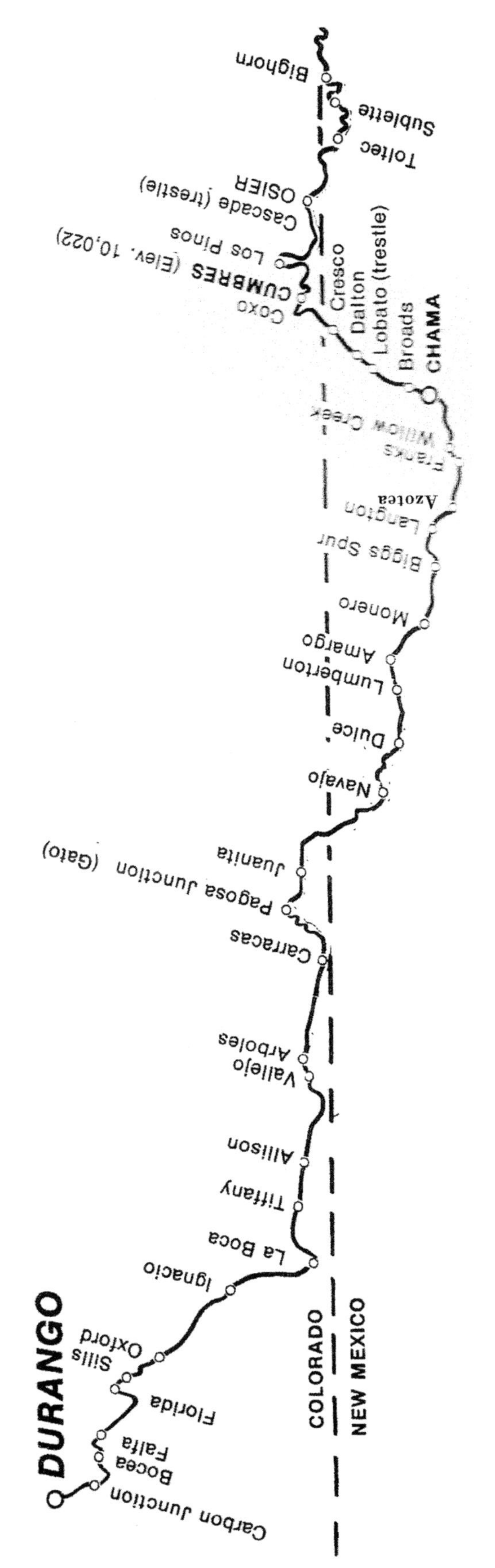

Tracking The D & RG - Chama To Durango

> Names on the maps of this territory rarely designate organized towns … [rather] they locate solitary outposts of civilization: section houses, water tanks, sidings, lumber mills, general stores, vanished stations, road crossings, or the decayed remains of a once prosperous village.[3]

So, who owned this wild, mostly uninhabited land which the D&RG crossed?

> Nobody knew for sure who owned the land- Jicarillas, Utes, Emmet Wirt, the Gomez family, the Sanchez family, or whether it was public domain. At the time no one cared much- the Rio Grande was in a hurry and the people wanted a railroad. When land ownership later was defined everybody got a little, even the (Jicarilla) Apaches.[4]

Constructing the San Juan Extension required thousands of wood cross ties on which to spike down the rails. Fortunately for the D&RG, the land was heavily forested:

> The cross ties used by the Denver & Rio Grande in 1880 were hand-hewn, six and one-half feet long by six inches square. A mile of track required 3,000 ties. [Thus the 245 miles from Alamosa to Silverton would require 735,000 ties.] Consequently, the coming of the railroad not only required the stripping of whole forests but gave birth to a permanent lumber industry to supply its needs alone.[5]

Hundreds of laborers were needed to cut down the trees and saw them into cross ties, and the D&RG advertised for help from as far away as Montreal, Canada:

> "Help Wanted: Good wood cutters interested in going to Colorado to earn from $3 to $5 a day hewing railroad ties from white pine. Obtain a contract signed by the Denver and Rio Grande Railway Company …" This newspaper advertisement appeared in a Montreal newspaper in April 1880. The French-Canadian sawyers (and Chinese laborers, and anyone else with a strong back) were needed to work on the famed San Juan Extension of the Rio Grande.[6]

The hewn cross ties had to be transported ahead of the advancing railroad in wagons hauled by horses or oxen. Thus, loggers tried to cut trees as close to the railhead as possible. Ties were not the only wood product the railroad needed. "Further millions of board feet of lumber went into culverts, trestles, bridges, water tanks and buildings along the railroad."[7] Mountainsides were stripped of timber to meet the needs of the railroad, and driving through the area today, one notices the scarcity of trees.

Building west from Chama in 1881, the track laying crews were hampered by snow:

> The bad weather of the winter of 1880–1881 that made construction over Cumbres Pass so difficult continued to plague the railroad builders west of Chama. By March 16, 1881, the end of track was only a little more than 15 miles beyond Chama.[8]

The track layers had successfully bridged Willow Creek and moved on to Azotea, just before the Continental Divide, which was only 10.33 miles west of Chama. This divide was significant in dividing watersheds, with waters on the east of it flowing to the Gulf of Mexico and Atlantic Ocean, and waters on the west of it flowing to the Pacific Ocean. The Continental Divide here had an elevation of 7,723 feet, which was lower than Chama's elevation of 7,863 feet. Thus, trains traveled downgrade from Chama to the divide. Strangely enough, the Continental Divide is not at Cumbres Pass (elevation 10,015 feet) as one might expect, but "just beyond Azotea, a shallow cut through an insignificant ridge, called Willow Creek Pass."[9] Also oddly, "the San Juan Extension was the first Rio Grande track to cross the Continental Divide, for it was to be about a month later before the Salida-Gunnison line did so."[10]

Some 5 miles west of Azotea, the railroad reached a point that would become known as Biggs, named after E. M. Biggs, president of the New Mexico Lumber Company, which had a sawmill here. Today, this is an important highway intersection with U.S. Highway 64 heading west to Dulce, and U.S. Highway 84 heading north to Chromo and Pagosa Springs, Colorado. From Biggs, the railroad headed west down into its first canyon—Monero Canyon. Here, the D&RG built a water tank, about 1 mile east of where the Monero depot was built.

> Early coal-fired engines had a coal-tender capacity of about fourteen tons and a water-storage capacity of about ten thousand gallons. Later engines could carry up to twenty-five tons and twenty thousand gallons. One pound of coal turned six pounds … of water to steam, so the railroad required far more water than coal. Locomotive storage capacities were based on two water stops to one fuel stop.[11]

Thus, water tanks needed to be spaced about every ten to twenty miles along the railroad to resupply the locomotive tenders. When the Willow Creek water tank was

Robert W. Richardson photographed K-37 no. 490 with a freight train crossing the Continental Divide just west of Azotea on November 11, 1955. (*Friends of the Cumbres & Toltec Scenic Railroad, Dorman Collection, RD009-059*)

torn down in 1900, the Monero tank became the first water tank west of Chama. The Monero tank was 19 miles from Chama. Coal was discovered at a mine in Monero, so this became a fuel stop as well as a water stop for the trains. The coal was also shipped out to other locations.

Just west of the settlement of Monero, Amargo Canyon begins with Amargo Creek flowing west.

> The railroad broke out of Monero Canyon toward the end of March [1881] and the town of Amargo was established as a temporary railhead ... Amargo was a typical end-of-rail conglomeration of tents, shacks and piles of construction material. It was occupied as a staging point for the drive to Durango.[12]

Soon after April 1, 1881, the track layers were ready to leave Amargo and head on toward Durango.

Just 3 miles west of Amargo, a few shacks were built, which eventually became the town of Lumberton. Lumberton became a very important point with logging railroads branching off to the north and to the south. As Lumberton grew, Amargo was abandoned and the log depot that had been built in Amargo was disassembled and transported farther west down the line to Gato.

Some 4 miles west of Lumberton the new town of Dulce was established. Dulce became the headquarters of the Jicarilla Apache Tribe, which had been located at Amargo prior to its demise. Navajo Canyon begins immediately west of Dulce, and the D&RG track layers encountered the Navajo River in the canyon four miles west. Here, track laying had to halt while a bridge was built across the Navajo River. A water tank (14 miles from the Monero tank) was constructed, along with a section house. Track laying was halted but grading was not. D&RG crews with tools and horses swam the Navajo River and started grading on the other side of the river. Eventually, the bridge across the river was completed, and the track layers could catch up with the grading crew. The track followed the Navajo River, crossing from New Mexico into Colorado.

In 9 miles, the Navajo River reached its confluence with the San Juan River. Here, another bridge had to be built. The previous process was repeated, with the grading crew swimming across the San Juan River while the track laying crew constructed the bridges necessary to get across the river. Shacks were thrown up to house the crews and this little settlement became Juanita, Colorado, which existed for another fifty years or so.

Some 4 miles west from Juanita, the railroad crews encountered a small settlement at Gato. This was a bit surprising as the land had been uninhabited for the 17 miles since Dulce. At Gato, a bridge had to be built across Gato Creek. A water tank, pump house, section house, and coaling facility were built here. When a logging railroad was built north from Gato to Pagosa Springs in 1899, the name of the village was changed to Pagosa Junction. When that railroad ceased to exist in 1935, the name was changed back to Gato.

From Gato, the rail line followed the San Juan River five miles west where a siding was built for passing trains. This siding became known as Carracas. From there, it was another 8 miles along the river to the settlement of Arboles. "The standard tank at Arboles was

Chama To Durango Water Tank Locations		
	Distance	Water
Location	Between	Source
	Locations	
Chama		Chama River
Willow Creek*	5 miles	Willow Creek
Monero	14 miles	Spring, 1 mi. so.
Navajo	14 miles	Navajo River
Pagosa Junction	13 miles	San Juan River
Arboles	13 miles	San Juan River
La Boca	15 miles	Pine River
Ignacio	7 miles	Pine River
Florida	12 miles	Florida River
Durango	14 miles	Animas River
*Willow Creek tank removed in 1900		

The Monero water tank, located about 1 mile east of the Monero depot, photographed by John W. Barriger III, *c. 1935.* (*Friends, Dorman Collection, RD009-040*)

The Lumberton depot served the D&RG after the Amargo depot was dismantled. This view to the east was captured by Gerald M. Best on September 3, 1952. (*Friends, Dorman Collection, RD009-065*)

Westbound K-37 no. 493 takes on water at the Navajo tank with its trailing freight cars on the 109-foot-long bridge over the Navajo River. Ernie Robart photographed it on October 3, 1967. (*Friends, Robart Collection, ERNG19671003-0410*)

Above: The three-span D&RG bridge over the San Juan River just west of Juanita on June 24, 1988, about twenty years after the abandonment of the line. The truss bridges are 185 feet and 126 feet long respectively, while the deck girder bridge is 64 feet. (*Photograph by the author*)

Right: The D&RG bridge across Gato Creek at Pagosa Junction still stands in May 2021, though trees and weeds are taking over the scene.

The La Boca bridge over the Pine River is still standing, as photographed by the author in May 2021, in this eastward view.

erected in 1887, although water had been manually pumped from the San Juan River since 1881."[13] When the tracks eventually reached Durango, freight trains had to be double-headed westbound because of the long ascending grade from Arboles to Falfa. The railroad left the San Juan River at Arboles and proceeded west to what would become the farming/ranching communities of Allison (7 miles from Arboles) and Tiffany (4 miles from Allison). From Tiffany (elevation 6,344 feet), the railroad followed Spring Creek four miles downstream between mesas to La Boca (elevation 6,177 feet). At La Boca, a water tank was built, along with a bridge across Los Pinos (Pine) River. The railroad then followed the Pine River north 7 miles, gaining elevation to Ignacio (6,437 feet).

Ignacio was the largest settlement the railroad had yet encountered. It was the headquarters of the Southern Ute Tribe, and a focal point for trade in southern Colorado. A station was constructed in Ignacio to handle passenger and freight traffic, but a water tank was not built until 1886. From Ignacio, the railroad climbed another 200 feet in 7 miles to Grommet (later named Oxford).

Climbing another 100 feet, the tracklayers reached Florida, 5 miles north of Grommet. Here the Florida River had to be bridged, and a water tank was constructed as it had been 19 miles since the last tank at La Boca. Proceeding north another 4 miles and 200 feet in elevation, the railroad reached Alfalfa (later named Falfa). Just west of Alfalfa, the railroad reached its highest point (6,958 feet) since crossing the Continental Divide in New Mexico. Then it began its 10-mile descent to Durango (elevation 6,520 feet). In 1905, Carbon Junction was constructed 2 miles south of Durango to handle the branch line to Farmington, New Mexico.

Animas City was a settlement two miles north of what would become Durango. It had been settled along the banks of the Animas River in the 1870s to supply food and building supplies to the silver mines 45 miles north at Silverton. Wagons and stagecoaches hauled people and goods to Silverton before the railroad was built. So why was Animas City not the terminus of the railroad rather than Durango? Durango historian and author Duane Smith explains:

> Durango might never have seen the light of day had not the ambitious Denver and Rio Grande Railroad clashed with a stubborn Animas City. The railroad's management planned to build through the valley and along the Animas Canyon to tap the rich mining district in the heart of the San Juan Mountains at Silverton. To do so, it had to go right past the small farming and ranching community of Animas City, two miles north of future Durango. The Rio Grande was willing to develop Animas City into a railroad center for a price and on its terms. Animas City would not stoop to either demand.[14]

Animas City refused the demands of the D&RG.

> [The railroad] then arranged for several loyal Rio Grande employees to homestead claims along the Animas downstream from Animas City. Soon after filing on these claims, the pseudo-homesteaders sold to the Durango Land and Coal Company [a subsidiary of the D&RG]. Durango was laid out on these plots and land sales began. Railroad facilities were plotted also, and some construction got under way. So, by the time the Narrow Gauge rolled into Durango it had a going town and some facilities to receive it.[15]

It was July 27, 1881, when the railroad finally rolled into Durango, whose name had been selected by former Colorado "territorial governor A.C. Hunt probably ... because of the location's similarity to Durango, Mexico, where he had just traveled on railroad business."[16]

K-28 no. 476 heading an eastbound freight out of Durango on November 9, 1967. The smelter smokestack can be seen in the upper mid-left in this photograph by Ernie Robart. (*Friends, Robart Collection, ERNG19671109-0133*)

2

Chama: Division Point on the D&RG

Cumbres Pass is at an elevation of 10,015 feet. The D&RG would have to descend 14 miles west and 2,152 feet from the pass to reach the budding village of Chama. The view downhill must have given pause to the railroad surveyors and track layers. It was a 4 percent grade that would have to be conquered.

> The fact that the line was indeed laid out and constructed by men using black powder, mules and dump carts is a shining example of the spirit of courage, farsightedness and perseverance with which our pioneer forebearers were endowed.[1]

The steep grade was not the only problem. Snow, and lots of it, slowed construction to Chama in 1880. The winters at Cumbres became notorious in the line's history. The winter of 1931 saw 496 inches of snow fall. "The line over Cumbres soon became known for its severe winters and heavy snow. Snow fences and sheds soon dotted the entire line from Antonito to Chama."[2]

> Chama was destined to become important to the railroad … The physical difficulties of building and maintaining a railroad over the mountains from Antonito on toward the west meant a sizable commitment for the railroad. The 4-percent grade from Chama to Cumbres Pass required extra [helper] locomotives to be stationed at Chama, with attendant repair and maintenance capabilities.[3]

With the arrival of the railroad, Chama boomed overnight.

> Chama was the major action facility between Alamosa and Durango. It functioned as a nerve center between the 2nd and 3rd districts, changing crews, adding helpers [engines], and feeding passengers over the years. Also housing crews, repairing

engines, and switching the yards for the local shippers made Chama a busy station.[4]

It was the presence of the railroad that proved to be Chama's saving grace. Chama's businesses were severely affected by the stock market crash of 1929, and then the winter of 1931 hit with ferocious blizzards. "Many sheepherders were wiped totally out due to the loss of their sheep … stores and businesses failed … Chama never again had the chance to be growth oriented."[5] Yet the railroad allowed Chama to survive. Locomotives had to be serviced; crews had to be fed and housed; and passengers needed lodging and food. With the establishment of the Cumbres & Toltec Scenic Railroad from Antonito to Chama in 1970, the same pattern holds true for Chama today.

Walking along Terrace Avenue in Chama today and looking down into the railyard, it is easy to imagine this is still the 1880s. From northeast to southwest, the yard is laid out much like it was originally. At the northeast end is the water tank and the oil-loading dock, and then the section house and coal tipple. Heading on south is the sand house, ash pit, and the roundhouse. Then comes the depot, the stockyards, and the wye. Currently, visitors are allowed to roam the yard, though visitation may be restricted at any time, particularly during train arrivals and departures.

D&RG trains coming down from Cumbres Pass to Chama had to first cross the Chama River on this two-span truss bridge at milepost 343.6. Cumbres & Toltec Scenic Railroad no. 487 crosses the bridge in June 2018.

K-28 no. 476 rests beside the depot in Chama on November 10, 1967. The D&RG and now the Cumbres & Toltec Scenic Railroad have been a lifeline for business in Chama, helping preserve the town. (*Photograph by Ernie Robart, Friends, Robart Collection, ERNG19671110-0023*)

The Chama depot in June 2018 is all spruced up in D&RG gold paint with brown trim. Notice that the "Chama" sign has been lowered beneath the upper window from its position above the window in the previous photograph.

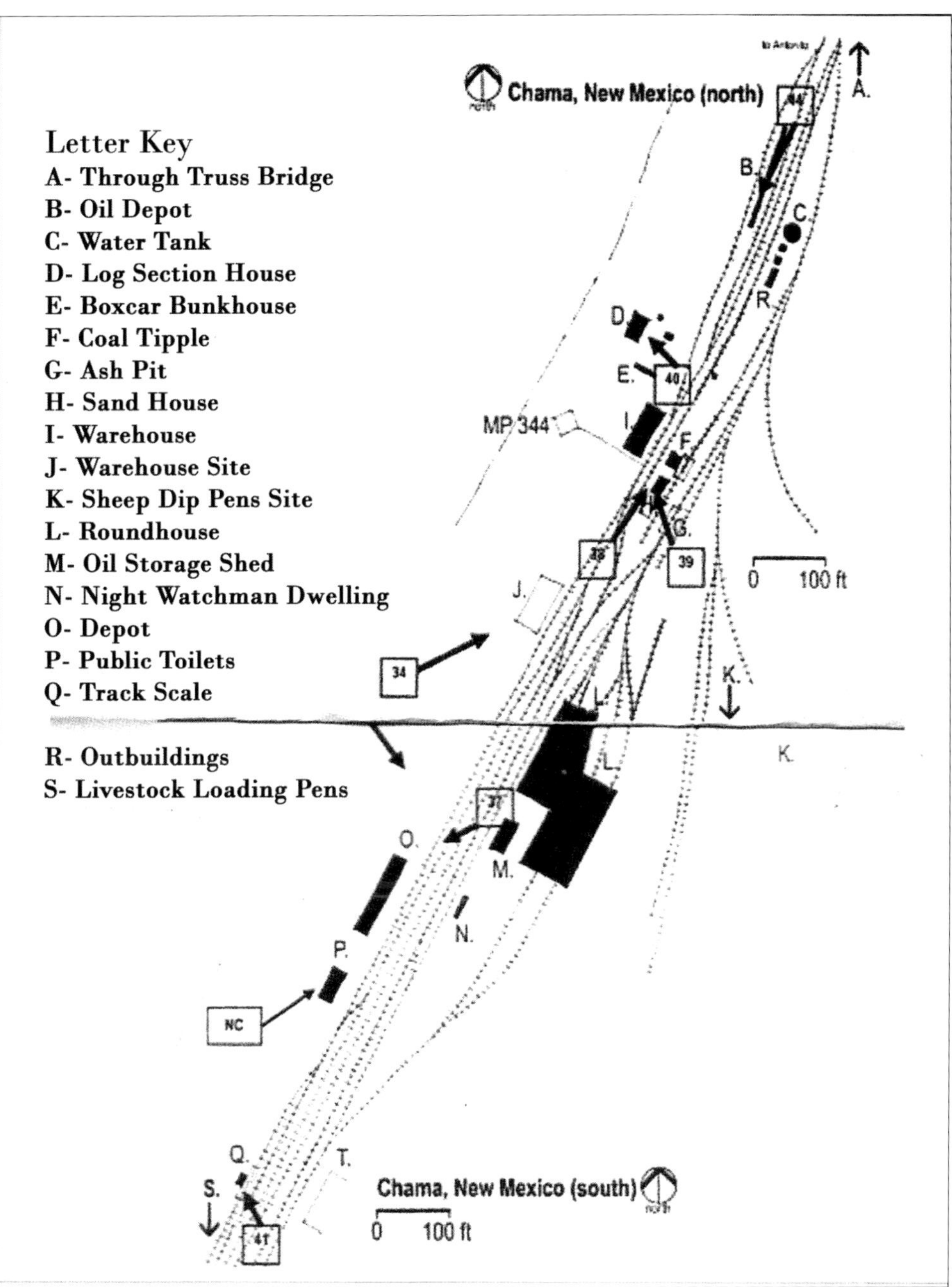

Chama rail yard diagram, 2007. (*National Park Service, National Register of Historic Places, www.catalog.archives.gov/id/84125714*)

The water tank at Chama is unusual in that it has two spouts to service locomotives on two tracks simultaneously. It is pump-fed from the Rio Chama ... The tank is representative of a standard D&RG design and holds 50,000 gallons in a wood structure on concrete foundations with a wood shingle roof. This structure was restored in 1994–1995.[6]

The coal tipple was built in 1924. Drop-bottom coal gondolas were pushed up an incline behind the tipple, and they released their load of coal into a bin below. From there, a two-bucket electric hoist lifted the coal to the top of the tower where the buckets dumped it into an opening at the top of the main bin. When locomotives stopped at the tipple for coal, it was released out the chute into the tender. The coal tipple is no longer used by the Cumbres & Toltec Scenic Railroad. Coal is loaded from a pile by a front-end loader into the tender. Across the tracks from the coal tipple is the restored 1880s log section house.

The oil-loading dock received its product from an oilfield just 6 miles north of the New Mexico–Colorado border and east of Chromo, Colorado. This oilfield was known as the "Gramps" field.

Gramps was the nickname for Lafayette Hughes, a Chama resident who owned [the] oilfield ... Multiple sources indicate that Hughes had "Gramps" painted on the cars so his grandchildren would know which car carried his oil.[7]

The oil was shipped in a pipeline downhill to Chama where it was stored in a "55,000 barrel and two 20,000-barrel storage tanks. Oil was then pumped from the storage tanks to the loading platform, and from there into waiting tank cars."[8] Hughes did not own his oil tank cars, but leased them from the Union Tank Car Company (UTLX). Hughes built a refinery in Alamosa to process his oil after it was shipped on the D&RG from Chama over Cumbres Pass to Alamosa.

Later, the refinery was sold to the Oriental Refining Company. It operated until closure in 1963, and it was dismantled in 1964. The Gramps tank cars were then scrapped. The Friends of the Cumbres & Toltec Scenic Railroad is in the process of restoring the oil loading dock, and the oil tank cars sitting on rails next to it.

Just south of the coal tipple is the sand house. Here sand was dried by a heater and loaded into the locomotive when needed. The engineer would release sand from the locomotive to the tracks to prevent slippage on steep grades or in wet or icy conditions. In later years, with less traffic on the line and proficient weed growth, sand was applied to the tracks when weeds caused slippage as the locomotive wheels passed over them. An ash pit was located next to the sand house. "An ash pit provided a place to clean the locomotive's firebox, carried out every four to six hours to rid it of the lumps of coal that did not burn completely."[9]

The original locomotive roundhouse in Chama was a six-stall wood structure built in 1882. It was served by a turntable that guided locomotives into a particular stall for service. This roundhouse burned down in the great Chama fire of 1899.

Above: This September 2019 view to the north in the Chama yard shows the two-spout water tank, the coal tower, and the sand house below it.

Right: View down the coal dump behind the coal tower. Drop-bottom gondola rail cars were pushed up a short slope and stopped here to release their coal load into the pit below. Then an electric bucket hoist would lift the coal and drop it into the bin at the top of the tower.

The restored log section house in the Chama yard is brightly lit by the early morning May sunshine in 2021.

Union Tank oil cars sit at the restored oil loading dock in the Chama yard in May 2021. Oil was pumped downhill through a pipeline from the "Gramps" oil field north of Chama to storage reservoirs below these pipes.

Six Union (UTLX) tank cars are spotted at the oil loading dock in Chama in May 2021. The D&RG moved loaded oil cars from here to the refinery in Alamosa.

Some of the leased Union tank cars were lettered "Gramps," signifying the originating oil field. (*Friends, Dorman Collection, RDS025-042*)

The sand house in the Chama yard still provides dried sand to the steam locomotives of the Cumbres & Toltec Scenic Railroad today.

> Then the present brick roundhouse [was built with] nine stalls. Four stalls were removed by the D&RG in 1936, and three more disappeared in the early 1950s, leaving only two stalls. Two new stalls were built by the C&TS in 1977.[10]

The turntable was removed in 1940, replaced by a wye at the south end of the yard to turn locomotives when necessary.

The original depot was built in 1882. It burned in the fire of 1899 and was rebuilt later that year. The function of the depot was to serve as a passenger waiting room with a telegrapher's office, station agent office, and a baggage and freight room. Today, the 1899 station still exists, housing a gift shop, ticket sales, and supply storage for the C&TS.

South of today's rail yard, the Friends of the Cumbres & Toltec Scenic Railroad have restored the 1888 cattle loading pens, and there is an excellent display here. Of particular interest are the ramps from the pens leading to double-decked chutes for loading sheep into double-decked cattle cars. Chama was a major sheep raising area particularly after the forests were logged off. "Sheep raising began on the open grasslands that gradually replaced the former lush forests. By the 1920s, there were about 50,000 head of sheep in the area, mostly raised by large landowners."[11] The severe winter of 1931–32 decimated the sheep herds, and cattle raising became

The original roundhouse in Chama burned down in 1899. It was replaced by a nine-stall brick roundhouse, two stalls of which remain on the right in the photograph. The two stalls on the left were added by the C&TS in 1977.

prominent after that. The restored cattle loading pens are located just off Highway 17 in the area within the wye.

The wye enables locomotives to change directions and eliminates the need for a turntable. The wye track is in the shape of a large triangle. There is a switch at each point of the triangle. The locomotive enters one leg of the triangle and goes beyond the triangle point, reverses, and backs into the switch, where it is switched down the next leg of the triangle, where it is switched again, and then goes forward on the final leg, thus changing the direction it was initially headed.

The oldest hotel in Chama is the Foster Hotel, built on Terrace Avenue in the early 1880s just west of the train station.

[It] was a home away from home for railroaders when they laid over on a run. It was also a lunch stop for train passengers for many years. In 1909 or 1910, the hotel was purchased by [Henry] Bert Foster, who operated the establishment as "Foster's Hotel" until 1946, when he was forced to sell because of poor health.[12]

The Foster Hotel was the only one of Chama's original commercial buildings to survive the fires of 1893, 1899, 1908, 1909, and 1925. It is listed on the National Register of Historic Places and is still open for business, mainly as a restaurant and bar. The fire of 1925 destroyed Foster's competitor hotel across the street, so Foster decided to expand his establishment.

The restored cattle loading pens at the extreme south end of the Chama yard. In the center of the photograph, a ramp is visible leading from the pens at the rear to the loading chutes at the front. There are two levels of the chute so that sheep could be loaded into the two levels of the stock car.

In May 2021, this sheep car was in the Chama yard. It is labeled "double deck" to distinguish it from the single-deck cattle cars.

The wye is located at the southern end of the Chama yard. Locomotives can make a three-point turn in the wye to change their direction of travel.

Within 2 years of the fire, Henry Foster had added the 2-story adobe section to the east of the existing hotel to expand his facilities to accommodate not only increasing railroad travelers, but also additional railroad workers. The adobe section added 6 guest rooms and 2 bathrooms to the Hotel. Still later, in 1932, Foster expanded further by adding the two-story frame structure approximately 25' north of the existing hotel, connecting it to the existing hotel by a two-story passage. The detached frame section added 9 guest rooms, 2 bathrooms and 4 apartments.[13]

Chama today has many motels, lodges, and RV parks, attesting to its success as a town based on tourism fostered by the Cumbres and Toltec Scenic Railroad. From Chama, we now begin tracking the D&RG line west to Durango.

Above: The two-story structure on the left is the Foster Hotel on Terrace Avenue in Chama seen in this *c.* 1910 photograph by an unknown photographer. By this time, it had survived four town fires, which left it the only 1880s commercial building still standing. (*National Park Service, National Register of Historic places, www.catalog.archives.gov/id/77847435*)

Below left: This is the original 1882 section of the Foster Hotel, which still serves today as a restaurant and hotel lobby. The rooms above are no longer used. The hotel rooms are now in the third building section to the north. To the right of the "Hotel Lobby" sign is where the adobe section facing Terrace Avenue was built in 1927.

Below right: This May 2021 view from milepost 344 in the Chama rail yard looks directly up the terrace to the adobe section of the Foster Hotel which was added on to the existing structure in 1927. It was 344 miles to Denver by rail from here.

3

Chama to Lumberton

From Chama west to Lumberton, you will be traveling along U.S. Highway 64/84. As you travel west, you can often see signs of the old railroad grade on the right (north) side of the highway, particularly noticeable near highway mile marker 154.

Heading west from Chama:

> Most "stations" were just passing sidings or tiny communities, the only places that warranted an agent in residence were Lumberton, Dulce, Gato and Ignacio … The train traveled through a region that had changed very little from the 1880s when the San Juan Extension was constructed.[1]

Some 5 miles west of Chama, the railroad builders encountered a creek which they named "Willow," undoubtedly because of the willow trees along its banks. A bridge was constructed across the creek and a water tank was also built. The water tank was torn down in 1900. Willow Creek was one of those places which was not a town, just a railroad siding with space for seventeen cars. Willow Creek flows south into the Chama River. Today's highway crosses it just east of mile marker 157.

Another 5 miles to the west, the community of Azotea was established. It was primarily a lumber camp named after a nearby large adobe ranch house with a flat roof (*azotea* in Spanish). Azotea was large enough to have a post office from 1887–1903. It had a siding capacity of thirty-two cars and was 0.4 miles east of the Continental Divide. The Continental Divide is at mile marker 152 and there is a historic marker on the south side of the highway. While there is no trace of Azotea today, there is a tunnel known as the Azotea Tunnel under the Continental Divide here, bringing water from the Navajo River in Colorado to Azotea Creek and Willow Creek and eventually to Heron Lake in New Mexico. The tunnel is thirteen miles long. It was completed in 1970 as part of the San Juan–Chama Diversion Project, which was designed to bring

The eastbound San Juan passenger train approaches the Willow Creek bridge *c.* 1950 on its way to Chama. (*Unknown photographer, Friends, Dorman Collection RD038-095*)

This May 2021 view shows the mountain range just north of Willow Creek as seen from U.S. Highway 64/84. The highway crosses Willow Creek just east of where this photograph was taken. Notice how the outline of the mountain range matches that of the previous photograph.

extra water to the Rio Grande watershed for the municipal water needs of Santa Fe, Albuquerque, and other communities.

Some 5 miles west of Azotea was the lumber camp of Biggs, located where today's U.S. Highway 64/84 divides with U.S. 84 going north to Chromo and Pagosa Springs Colorado, and U.S. 64 going west to Monero, Amargo, Lumberton, and Dulce. Biggs was named after E. M. Biggs, a resident of Chama who became president of the New Mexico Lumber Company which was incorporated on December 16, 1892. Biggs had a siding capacity of nineteen cars.

Coal was discovered 4 miles west of Biggs as the D&RG was constructed through a canyon. A settlement known as Monero grew up around the coal mine, and the canyon was also called Monero. The name "Monero" comes from an Italian word meaning "money." Many of the coal miners at Monero were of Italian descent. "In 1885, a standard 50,000-gallon tank was erected at Monero. The water source was a spring over a mile away to the south."[2]

> The town had a one-room school, a store, a saloon, a Catholic church, and a Penitente morada. The population reached a peak in the 1930s. There were two large mines and several smaller ones being worked 24 hours a day ... By the 1960s the mines were closing down.[3]

The Penitente morada was one of the many church-like structures built in Northern New Mexico to serve the area's far-flung Catholic population.

> There were never enough Catholic priests to serve the congregation of each village. Lay groups of devout local men [Penitentes] were formed to fill in for priests, conducting prayer services, saying the rosary, tending the sick, and burying the dead ... From the 1700s, Penitente groups practiced self-flagellation during Holy Week. Because of this, in the 1850s, Archbishop Lamy of Santa Fe wanted the brotherhood banned ... The Vatican banned the brotherhood in 1889 ... It was finally recognized again in 1947, when Archbishop Edwin Byrnes of Santa Fe allowed the group to continue, as long as members promised to stop the rite of self-flagellation.[4]

Monero had a post office from 1884–1963 when the mining activity had all but ceased. Today, Monero is a ghost town with fewer remaining buildings every year. Highway construction on U.S. 64 has routed the road high above Monero Canyon today, and after crossing the new bridge headed west, you will have to park on the right side of the highway and climb the steep embankment to catch a glimpse of Monero below. With its large coal-mining operations, Monero had a siding capacity of sixty-three cars to accommodate the many coal gondolas loaded here.

As the D&RG pulled out of the settlement of Monero, it then entered Amargo Canyon. *Amargo* is the Spanish word for "bitter," describing the taste of the water in Amargo Creek flowing through the canyon. Some 3 miles west of Monero, the D&RG set up a tent camp for construction workers, naming it Amargo.

Above: A K-28 leads the eastbound San Juan passenger train at Azotea siding on Christmas day, 1948. (*Photograph by Robert Richardson, Friends, Dorman Collection, RD009-068*)

Below left: View east at the Continental Divide along U.S. Highway 64/84 in May 2021 about 0.4 miles west of Azotea. Various publications list the elevation here from 7,272 feet to 7,275 feet.

Below right: The roads along the former D&RG San Juan Extension are now recognized as the Tracks Across Borders Scenic Byway in Colorado and New Mexico. The view here is to the east just beyond the Continental Divide at Azotea.

K-36 no. 483 crossing U.S. Highway 64/84 at Biggs as it pulls the westbound final Rocky Mountain Railroad Club excursion to Durango on May 28, 1966. (*Photograph by Ernie Robart, Friends, Robart Collection, ERNG019660528-0373*)

This is the highway intersection at Biggs in May 2021. U.S. 64 heads west on the left, and U.S. 84 heads north on the right. The D&RG followed the western route 4 miles to Monero from here.

Above: K-36 no. 483 crosses U.S. Highway 64 on May 28, 1966, as it enters Monero Canyon, pulling the final Rocky Mountain Railroad Club excursion to Durango. (*Photograph by Ernie Robart, Friends, Robart Collection, ERNG19660528-0403*)

Left: K-36 no. 487 pulls a westbound freight train across U.S. Highway 64 on June 13, 1967, heading into Monero Canyon. (*Photograph by Ernie Robart, Friends, Robart Collection, ERNG19670613-0353*)

This westbound view shows U.S. Highway 64 entering Monero Canyon in May 2021. The D&RG would have crossed the highway just before this point and would be traveling along the grade seen in the middle right.

K-36 no. 487 at the left with another K-36 leading a freight train on the right at the coal dock in Monero on November 6, 1949. (*Photograph by Robert Richardson, Friends, Dorman Collection, RD009-037*)

Above: The remains of a coal dock can be seen at Monero in this May 2021 photograph by the author. The view is northwest.

Below left: A closeup of the remains of a coal dock at Monero in May 2021, with the remains of a boiler on the ground and an abandoned structure.

Below right: The west end of Monero Canyon as the D&RG railroad grade travels through the cut in the rocks to enter Amargo Canyon at the left in this 2021 view.

Amargo was a tent city catering to the needs of the rough railroad construction crews. Card sharks, gamblers, confidence men, and prostitutes contributed to the lawless atmosphere. A self-styled band of desperadoes headed by Charley Allison set up tents on Amargo's outskirts and proceeded to terrorize the surrounding countryside. A year earlier, Allison had been a deputy sheriff in Conejos [Colorado].[5]

Other trouble came to Amargo as soon as the first tents were set up. There was a skirmish with a "small band of ... Apaches ... there is no record that any blood was shed."[6] When things settled down, Amargo became an important railhead for the D&RG as it headed west, and a siding was built with a capacity of thirty cars. In 1888, Ernest Ingersoll traveled on the D&RG passenger train to Durango. Arriving at Amargo he wrote that, "we found several hundred Apaches waiting to receive their rations, it being the weekly issuing day."[7] Amargo served as the headquarters for the Jicarilla Apache Nation until Dulce was founded.

Amargo Canyon is on private property today. The canyon cannot be viewed from U.S. 64. As Amargo Creek flows west out of the canyon into Amargo Park, there is a dirt road leading back into the canyon. The author was fortunate to meet the landowner driving out on this road. Permission was obtained to drive back to their home and hike the railroad grade up the canyon. This was a remarkable experience as there are bridge pilings over Amargo Creek (which was shallow enough for us to jump across) and many railroad ties. Hiking up the canyon, an unforgettable view of Table Rock was discovered, which allowed comparison with the 1908 photograph of D&RG locomotive 206 posing there.

Just 3 miles from Amargo Canyon, U.S. 64 will take you to the town of Lumberton. In September 1893, E. M. Biggs purchased the following:

Forty acres of land along the D& RG [three] miles west of Amargo, and planned to lay part of it off in town lots and establish a mill there ... The new town would be called Lumberton ... "Railway Age" ... said that the D&RG planned to move the Amargo depot there, for the birth of Lumberton signaled the death of Amargo ... By July 19 [1895] the Amargo depot building ... was being torn down and removed to Lumberton.[8]

It is not clear if the Amargo depot was moved to Lumberton and then to Gato, or if it was moved directly from Amargo to Gato. While the birth of Lumberton did indeed bring about the demise of Amargo, Lumberton soon had its own problems. Biggs built a sawmill there, but soon found that there was a lack of adequate water supply in Lumberton. Sawmills of that time period depended on water to heat in boilers producing steam which generated electricity to run the saws. Lumberton was located on Amargo Creek which ran dry for a good portion of the year. After two years of frustration with the water supply in Lumberton, Biggs moved his sawmill to Chama. "Lumberton thus declined as a lumber processing center, but rather than disappearing took on a new importance as a railroad junction point."[9]

K-36 no. 483 leads the Rocky Mountain Railroad Club return trip east from Durango on May 30, 1966. The sign identifies the U.S. 64 highway bridge crossing Amargo Creek. (*Unidentified photographer, Friends, Dorman Collection, RDS051-014*)

This is the view east in May 2021 up the private road into Amargo Canyon from U.S. Highway 64. The Rocky Mountain Railroad Club excursion train in the previous photograph would have followed this grade east into the canyon.

On the private property in Amargo Canyon, the D&RG railroad ties point the way to the remains of a trestle across Amargo Creek. The trestle posts can be seen in the upper middle of this photograph by the author in May 2021.

Throughout the private ranch in Amargo canyon where the author was given permission to explore, railroad ties can be found along the D&RG grade. This is the view east up the canyon.

D&RG locomotive no. 206 poses for a photograph at Table Rock in Amargo Canyon in April 1908. (*Photograph by George Barbor, Friends, Payne Collection, AMP01-046*)

This May 2021 view is at the spot where D&RG locomotive 206 posed for a photograph at Table Rock in 1908. The distinctive rock formations at the top are still there. This view toward the west shows the railroad grade going from the sagebrush at the right into the cut between the trees at the left.

Logging railroads branched off north and south from Lumberton. The Rio Grande and Pagosa Springs Railroad was constructed north in 1895. Although it ended a few miles south of Pagosa Springs, this railroad shipped out logs until the supply of timber diminished in 1914. South of Lumberton the Rio Grande and Southwestern Railroad was constructed in 1903, reaching 42 miles southeast to El Vado and Gallinas Mountain. It remained in operation until 1924. When the logging railroads ceased operation, Lumberton entered a gradual decline until it was surpassed by Dulce in size and importance.

Lumberton townsfolk await the arrival of the train at the depot, *c.* 1940s. U.S. Highway 64 is to the left of the tracks in this westward view. (*Unknown photographer, Friends, Dorman Collection, RDS020-010*)

U.S. Highway 64 enters Lumberton in this May 2021 view to the west. The skyline approximates the view above the depot in the previous photograph.

K-36 no. 483 pulls the westbound Rocky Mountain Railroad Club excursion train across U.S. Highway 64 in Lumberton on May 28, 1966. (*Photograph by Ernie Robart, Friends, Robart Collection, ERNG19660528-0543*)

4

Lumberton to Pagosa Junction

Just 4 miles west of Lumberton, the town of Dulce grew up around the homestead of Jose Eugenio Gomez, who had settled there in 1877 because of the availability of "sweet water" (*agua dulce* in Spanish). As opposed to the bitter water of Amargo and Lumberton, the sweet water arose in a spring 4 miles south of what would become the settlement of Dulce. In 1887, President Grover Cleveland signed an executive order creating the Jicarilla Apache reservation. The reservation extended from the Colorado border south to Cuba, New Mexico, and surrounded the small town of Dulce. When the D&RG built the San Juan Extension through here in 1881, neither the town of Dulce nor the reservation existed. As Dulce grew, thanks in large part to the railroad, it became the headquarters of the Jicarilla Apache Nation, replacing Amargo. *Jicarilla* means small bowl or basket in Spanish, and this group of Apache took the name Jicarilla "referring to the small, sealed baskets they used as drinking vessels."[1]

The reservation totals 742,315 acres, and has a population of about 3,500, with 2,500 living in Dulce. The D&RG built a station in Dulce and a siding with a capacity of 67 cars. Arriving in Dulce on U.S. Highway 64 today, you will proceed west through town. When the highway curves left, turn right on Narrow Gauge Street. This will take you past the two deteriorating D&RG cattle cars on the old siding.

Proceeding west on Narrow Gauge Street, you soon enter Navajo Canyon and in 4 miles will reach the Navajo River. Here, the D&RG bridge over the river is preserved, as is the water tank at the west end of the bridge. There was a section house at Navajo, and a siding accommodating twenty-three cars. This area was inhabited by some Navajo natives prior to the establishment of the Jicarilla Apache reservation.

The pavement ends just west of the Navajo River crossing, and the dirt road (J9) continues along the bank of the river as it flows northwest to the San Juan River. This road is extremely rutted and rough. It should not be attempted when it is wet and muddy. Be forewarned—you will probably get stuck. In about 5 miles, you will reach the Colorado border, and the road becomes much better from this point on.

Above: The view west at Dulce, *c.* 1940, showing the station and the siding. (*Unknown photographer, Friends, Dorman Collection, RDS060-018*)

Below left: The view west at Dulce had changed when Ernie Robart took this photograph on June 5, 1965. The station is gone, but the siding remains. Narrow Gauge Street is to the left of the siding. (*Friends, Robart Collection, ERNG19650607-0140*)

Below right: This is the same view west at Dulce as the previous two photographs, however it is now May 2021. Only a part of the siding remains with two D&RG cattle cars parked there. Narrow Gauge Street is on the left.

The Navajo water tank and bridge are seen in this view to the east taken by the author on June 24, 1988. Members of the Rocky Mountain Railroad Club are exploring the scene.

In May 2021, the Navajo water tank and bridge are still standing on the Jicarilla Apache Reservation.

In Colorado, you will be on County Road 551 as you continue to follow the D&RG grade along the Navajo River. You are now on the Southern Ute Indian Reservation. The Utes originally settled in the San Juan Mountains farther to the north, but after the Civil War, clashes between incoming white settlers and miners with the Utes increased substantially. Cries among the newcomers arose that "the Utes must go!" The Brunot Treaty of May 21, 1873, accomplished just that:

> 3.5 million acres of land were opened for legal entry by miners and settlers ... the Utes still had 15,500,000 acres of land in Colorado Territory. When the Brunot Treaty was signed, the Utes lost their sacred San Juan Mountains in return for a guaranteed reservation ... along the Colorado-New Mexico boundaries.[2]

Some 4 miles into Colorado, you will come to the ghost town of Juanita on the right side of the road. About all that is left here are the adobe remains of a church and a boarded-up building that was a school. Just to the north of the school is the Juanita cemetery. The D&RG built a section house, bunk house, and siding for twenty-three cars here. There were also stock pens for loading cattle. Cattle raising continues in the area today.

From Juanita, the road continues north and crosses the San Juan River. After crossing the bridge, turn left onto County Road 550. The D&RG did not make this crossing. The railroad continued west along the Navajo River until its confluence with the San Juan River and then made its often-photographed crossing of the San Juan River over a three-span bridge. Road 550 will take you on a very steep climb above the San Juan River. There is a large pull-out near the top of the road where you can walk out and gaze upon the D&RG bridges far below.

Some 4 miles west of Juanita, Road 550 makes a sharp descent around a curve and the remains of Pagosa Junction come into view. Here you will be back along the railroad grade, with track, a siding and the D&RG bridge over Gato Creek. *Gato* is Spanish for "cat," so the creek was also known as Cat Creek. The creek flows into the San Juan River. When a logging railroad (the Rio Grande, Pagosa and Northern) was built from here north to Pagosa Springs in 1899, the name of the settlement was changed from Gato to Pagosa Junction. When the logging railroad ceased operations in 1935, the name was changed back to Gato.

At Gato, the D&RG built a section house, pump house, water tank, and a seventy-five-car siding. The station was brought in from Amargo. A post office was opened in Pagosa Junction in 1899, and the population was roughly 200. With the activity from the logging railroad, the town population increased to 447 in 1930. When Pagosa Junction became Gato again in 1935, the population started declining. On November 30, 1954, the post office closed. In September 1962, the school closed as there were only seventeen students left.

The author first visited Pagosa Junction on a field trip with the Rocky Mountain Railroad Club in June 1988. At the time, it was fairly well-preserved. The water tank was standing, there was a gondola car on the siding, and the Gomez Store was sitting right next to the siding. The store had been closed since 1971, but much of

This *c.* 1950 view at Juanita shows the main line, siding, and a boxcar storage facility. (*Unknown photographer, Friends, Dorman Collection, RDS026-052*)

Ernie Robart took this photograph at Juanita from the rear of the westbound Alamosa Kiwanis Kolor Karavan excursion train on September 30, 1966. This was the final passenger excursion train on the D&RG. Regular passenger service had ended in 1951. (*Friends, Robart Collection, ERNG19660930-0733*)

Above left: In June 1988, this church was standing in Juanita as members of the Rocky Mountain Railroad Club passed by on their field trip.

Above right: In May 2021, the Juanita church stood in ruins at the right of the author's photograph. The old school building is still standing on the left.

Below: On August 25, 1966, Ernie Robart photographed this eastbound D&RG freight headed by engine no. 492 crossing the triple bridge over the San Juan River, west of Juanita. (*Friends, Robart Collection, ERNG19660825-0260*)

Above left: The triple bridge over the San Juan River still stands as seen by the author in May 2021. The longest span to the left is 185 feet, while the middle span is 126 feet long. The deck girder span on the right is 64 feet long.

Above right: This view to the west, *c.* 1940, shows the complete layout of Pagosa Junction. The San Juan River is on the left. Toward the top right is the D&RG bridge over Gato Creek. Just to the right front of the bridge is the Gomez Store. There are several gondola cars on the siding. The station is in between the siding and the main line. An eastbound freight train is taking on water at the tank. The pump house is ahead of the train on the river side. Section houses are at the lower right front. (*Photograph from the Center of Southwest Studies, Fort Lewis College*)

Below: There is considerably less action in Pagosa Junction on June 24, 1988, than in the previous photograph. This view to the west shows the water tank (which collapsed in 2006), the Gomez Store on the right, and the bridge across Gato Creek. Members of the Rocky Mountain Railroad Club explored the site.

the merchandise, particularly canned goods, remained inside. The owner even gave us a tour inside the store. In 2000, Lilliosa Padilla and her son Ray were the only two residents left in Pagosa Junction. "Felix Gomez, Lilliosa's father, had closed the doors on the Gomez Store in 1971, leaving its contents intact. Since then, Mrs. Padilla has conducted guided tours of the historic building and its contents."[3]

When the Southern Ute Tribe refused to renew the Padilla leases on the land in 2000, they were forced to leave. They sold their house and moved the Gomez Store "to Pagosa Springs ... to become part of a museum collection at the Fred Harman Art Museum."[4] Unfortunately, now the Harman Museum is defunct and in May 2021, the Gomez Store sat forlornly propped on moving girders, as if searching for a new location. At its height in the early 1930s, Pagosa Junction had "a lumber mill with a large payroll, a hotel, restaurant, boarding houses, stables, school, post office, at least two general stores, Catholic church, possibly a newspaper, and perhaps other businesses."[5]

In summer 2006, the water tank at Pagosa Junction collapsed. As the remains of Pagosa Junction continue to deteriorate, the Southern Ute tribe seems to have no interest in preservation, and the tribe has posted "No Trespassing" signs all over the site.

> It was once called Gato, Pagosa Junction was, and like its namesake—the cat—it has had nine lives. Now that the Padilla family is moving out, the old river village and railroad town is empty. For the first time since 1880 and maybe earlier, Pagosa Junction has no residents. The move has moistened more than one cheek with a silent tear shed in memory of an almost forgotten past ... Is Pagosa Junction dead, or do one or more of the nine lives remain? Only time will tell.[6]

Perhaps with the creation of the Tracks Across Borders Scenic Byway in Colorado and New Mexico in 2015, there is one more life left for Pagosa Junction. The byway runs from Durango to Chama, following the D&RG San Juan Extension right through Pagosa Junction. The purpose of the byway is as follows:

> To maintain, market and promote the Tracks Across Borders Byway as a 'long museum' over the pathways of the past so that travelers develop an understanding and appreciation of the rich railroad, cultural, historical, recreational, agricultural and natural features of the byway that have endured and continues today. To make navigation easy and match visitor preferences and expectations to the byway itself. Encourage and promote healthy and diverse tourism that helps communities and businesses along the byway thrive.[7]

If the byway is to be a "long museum," one would think that preservation of Pagosa Junction would be a major goal. Thus far, nothing has been accomplished in that regard.

On June 24, 1988, members of the Rocky Mountain Railroad Club strolled through Pagosa Junction. There was an abandoned gondola car on the siding at the right, with the Gomez Store and the D&RG bridge in the distance.

The Gomez Store was still in pretty good shape on June 24, 1988, sitting on the siding at Pagosa Junction. Owner Lilliosa Padilla and her son gave us a tour inside the store.

In May 2021, the author viewed the abandoned Gomez Store resting on steel girders on the grounds of the defunct Harman Museum in Pagosa Springs. The store had been moved here in 2000 from Pagosa Junction.

St. John the Baptist Church was built in Pagosa Junction in 1927. It still stands on a hillside above the abandoned village. An annual mass is still held in the church.

Above left: The water tank at Pagosa Junction collapsed in the summer of 2006, covering what used to be the D&RG main line. This May 2021 view was seen by the author.

Above right: A D&RG gondola car sits abandoned on the siding at Pagosa Junction in May 2021. The bridge is barely visible in the trees beyond the curve in the track.

Below: The siding from the right joins the D&RG main line just before it enters the bridge over Gato Creek in this May 2021 view. The Gomez Store stood just to the right of the siding.

Above left: The D&RGW RR logo is seen in May 2021 stenciled on a steel girder at the Gato Creek bridge in Pagosa Junction. Similar stencils can be seen on the bridges at La Boca and at Florida farther west on the line.

Above right: This view to the west in May 2021 shows the emptiness of the once-bustling Pagosa Junction site.

Below left: The view east at Pagosa Junction in May 2021 shows the main line with the remains of a section house on the left and the pump house on the right. How much longer will these buildings remain standing without preservation efforts?

Below right: Hope for the preservation of Pagosa Junction may lie with the cooperation of the Ute Indian Tribe with the Tracks Across Borders Scenic Byway Commission. The byway sign is seen at the Colorado border heading north from New Mexico in May 2021.

5

Pagosa Junction to Durango

Continuing the drive west on County Road 500 from Pagosa Junction, the road winds along the canyon of the San Juan River. "For five miles west of Gato, the railroad was built above the high- water marks (of the San Juan) along sandstone and shale hillsides."[1] Finally, after 5 miles, the canyon widens out into a broad plain, and it was here that the Carracas siding was constructed. *Carraca* is a Spanish word for a type of rattle used in Catholic worship services (particularly by the Penitente Brotherhood) during Holy Week. It is unknown why the siding here was named Carracas, but the nearby mesa is also known as Carracas. The siding accommodated thirty-nine cars, and it was the spot where the eastbound and westbound San Juan passenger trains passed each other daily. In 1987, author Richard Dorman noted:

[Carracas is] just a wide spot in the road. The telephone booth, sign and the indication of where the tracks ran have all disappeared. Today nothing shows it was an active passing meet for the D&RGW's prestigious passenger trains. Every day at 1:35 in the afternoon the two little trains passed on their eastbound and westbound missions. No more![2]

In 2021, Carracas is the site of oil and gas operations that have increased in number with the prevalence of fracking in Archuleta and La Plata Counties.

D&RG passenger service to Durango was initiated as soon as the rails reached there on July 27, 1881. After 1910, the passenger train became known as "The San Juan," as proclaimed on the drumhead at the rear of the train and in D&RG timetables. Toward the end of the Great Depression, the equipment on the narrow-gauge passenger line between Alamosa and Durango was in sad shape. It was in desperate need of refurbishing. "Management started a refurbishing program that cost $79, 526 … The project was finished in 1937, and the San Juan sister trains were unveiled for service

On October 8, 1945, the D&RG westbound San Juan passenger train was waiting to meet the eastbound San Juan at Carracas. (*Photograph by Robert Richardson, Friends, Dorman Collection, RD168-0108*)

The San Juan sister trains meet at Carracas on March 19, 1950. (*Photograph by John Maxwell, Friends, Dorman Collection, RDS060-005*)

This westward view at Carracas in 2021 shows no sign of San Juan trains or D&RG tracks.

The view east at Carracas in 2021 shows the prevalence of the oil and gas industry in Archuleta and La Plata counties today. Note the pipeline in the center of the photograph.

between Alamosa and Durango."[3] These were the eastbound and westbound trains that met in Carracas every day.

The D&RG bragged about the San Juan in their 1937 publicity brochure:

> The San Juan operating between Alamosa and Durango, are modern vestibuled trains, steam heated and equipped with 110-volt current. Smartly appointed are the coaches and lounges. In fact, no globe trotter can claim he has been everywhere until he has traveled over the Rio Grande's narrow gage system.[4]

The San Juan was still in beautiful shape in 1947, as Lucius Beebe gushingly wrote in *Holiday Magazine*:

> It is one of the most beautiful trains in the world ... The cars are dark green and gold ... The chair car is a miniscule version of all train luxury in a single unit, its walls paneled with white birch, its lighting fixtures plated with silver from Colorado's own mines ... Its tiny kitchen is the last word in metal modernity, with electric stove and ice boxes.[5]

With all this luxury, who could complain that it took nine hours for the train to cover the 200 miles between Alamosa and Durango?

This preserved drumhead of the San Juan passenger train is displayed here at the end of the parlor car on the Cumbres and Toltec Scenic Railroad excursion train on June 18, 2021.

The schedules between Alamosa and Durango were such as to permit passengers to have daylight through the most scenic part of the 200-mile trip. The schedule time of nine hours was not bad considering grades and curvatures.[6]

The San Juan train no. 215 westbound was scheduled to leave Alamosa at 7 a.m., depart Chama at 11.15 a.m., and arrive in Durango at 4.05 p.m. The eastbound no. 216 left Durango at 11.15 a.m., departed Chama at 4 p.m., and arrived in Alamosa at 8.30 p.m. The trains met in Carracas at 1.35 p.m.

Robert Richardson, founder of the Colorado Railroad Museum, described the San Juan consist in his book *Chasing Trains*:

> During the summer season, the San Juan consisted of five cars: an RPO-express car, a baggage car, two vestibuled coaches and a "first class" parlor-dinette car. During the winter months there usually was a four-train consist, with one less coach. Motive power usually was a class K-28 470 series outside frame 2-8-2. The parlor car, of course, was popular with tourists, who gladly paid the small extra fare for one of the reserved first-class seats. The dinette at the end of the train served meals at prices that were in effect when the San Juan was modernized in 1937.[7]

Coming out of the Great Depression though, not a lot of people had extra money to pay for a luxury train ride. After World War II, people did have money, but they spent it on automobiles and a fast ride, not the slow train ride. Ridership on the San Juan never met expectations and steadily declined. The D&RG decided to get out of the passenger business (except for the Durango to Silverton line), and the last San Juan train ran in a snowstorm on January 31, 1951. "The New Mexico legislature had not officially approved the abandonment of the passenger service yet, so a train was run in the New Mexico portion of the trackage until May 22, 1951."[8] The consist for this train, which ran between Dulce and Chama, was locomotive K-28 no. 473, tender, and combine coach no. 212.[9] The train was backed from Dulce to the wye at Lumberton, where it was turned for the remainder of the journey to Chama. It was a rather sad ending for a glamorous narrow-gauge passenger train (see image on page 66).

Continuing west from Carracas, County Road 500 follows the San Juan River to the point where it flows into Navajo Lake. Navajo Lake was formed by a dam built on the San Juan River from 1958 to 1962. The new lake forced the relocation of the D&RG tracks, as well as the relocation of the town of Arboles, which would be flooded by the lake. The creation of Navajo Lake was part of the Colorado River Storage Project, which built dams on the major tributaries of the Colorado River in order to provide electric power and water supplies to towns of the Southwest and to the Navajo Reservation. The relocation of the D&RG tracks along the east side of the lake added 4 miles to the journey to Durango and necessitated the building of a new bridge across the Piedra River.

On July 7, 1959, Bureau of Reclamation and D&RGW Railroad officials inspected the proposed alignment for relocation of the railroad around the upper end of the Navajo Reservoir. Reclamation awarded a contract for initial stages of the relocation

On April 22, 1951, Robert Richardson photographed the downsized San Juan passenger train at the wye in Lumberton. This short train ran between Dulce and Chama from February 1, 1951, until May 22, 1951, when the New Mexico legislature granted abandonment of passenger service on the line. (*Friends, Dorman Collection, RD009-088*)

of the line the following year on October 23, 1960, to Colorado Constructors, Inc. The contractor, responsible for earthwork and structures relocation, began work the same day. Reclamation accepted all work on the contract as completed on July 20, 1961. Reclamation awarded the contract for ballasting and track laying on March 7, 1962 ... and accepted the contract as complete on September 7, 1962.[10]

Creation of Navajo Lake meant the inundation of four small Hispanic communities—Los Pinos, Rosa, and Los Martinez in New Mexico, and Los Arboles in Colorado.

Around 1958, officials with the Bureau of Reclamation started showing up. "They came to us and said they were going to buy our land," says Jose [Ed] Marquez. "If you refused to sell, they would just condemn your place and tear it down anyway. They bought you out, gave you so much time, and you had to pack up your little rags and leave." Some residents hired a man from Farmington to load their houses onto trailers, then drive them, one-by-one, down the road into nearby towns such as Allison, Ignacio and what's now called "New Arboles."[11]

Journeying on the reconstructed County Road 500 along Navajo Lake today, you will essentially be following the route of the D&RG tracks. Navajo State Park has several recreation sites located here, named after railroad terms such as "S-Curves" and "Narrow Gauge Junction." Just past Narrow Gauge Junction, Road 500 joins Colorado Highway 151. Take a left turn here and soon cross the highway bridge over the Piedra River. If traffic allows, slow down and look to the south and you will see the D&RG bridge still standing over the Piedra River.

> Perhaps the most outstanding feature [of the track relocation] from the railfan photographer's standpoint, is the 277-foot, 3-span bridge over the Piedra, which should present a fine setting for snapping the occasional freights, and even more occasional excursion passenger trains, using the line ... A sour note, aside from the fact that any "progress" is bound to be resented by the traditionalists ... was provided when the huge girders for the bridge were brought in by truck![12]

Also, fortunately for the railfan photographer, Navajo State Park has preserved the bridge in its watchable wildlife viewing area as a pedestrian bridge over the Piedra River. Watch for the sign on CO151 soon after driving over the highway bridge and turn left into the area. Park and walk the short trail to the bridge. As you walk across it, imagine a D&RG steam locomotive and freight train barreling through in 1962.

Continue driving on CO151 until you reach the entrance Road 982 to Navajo State Park. Turn left here, passing some of the residences of "New Arboles."

> *Los Arboles* is Spanish for "the trees" and acquired its name from the nearby groves along the Piedra and San Juan Rivers. The community grew on the peninsula of land between the two rivers where the narrow-gauge Denver & Rio Grande Western Railroad bridged the Piedra. The town was apparently created by the coming of the railroad in 1881.[13]

However, the settlers at Los Arboles were removed from the land in 1882 because they were on Ute Indian Reservation land. After that, the "town" simply became a stop for the D&RG. It was not until 1899 that settlers returned after the passage of the Dawes Act, which allowed settlers on lands that had not been appropriated by the Utes.

> Los Arboles grew into a transportation center for shipping cattle and sheep from both Colorado and New Mexico. There were large corrals by the depot and dipping vats. The sheep coming in from New Mexico had to be dipped to kill any parasites before they continued on to the Denver market.[14]

As you continue on the road toward the Navajo State Park entrance, you will see the D&RG water tank standing on a hill in the distance. At the base of the hill, turn left to view the water tank.

> The standard tank at Arboles was erected in 1887, although water had been manually pumped from the San Juan River since 1881 ... The old tank was replaced by a 12,000-gallon steel tank in 1949. It was an old locomotive tender placed on a concrete foundation ... The water service was retired in 1964.[15]

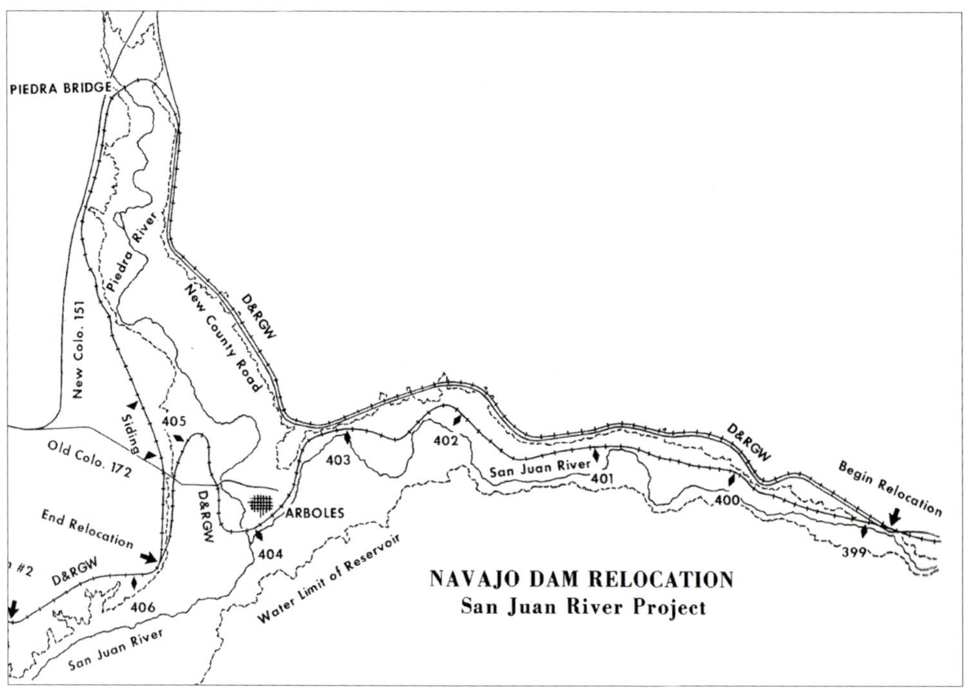

Creation of the Navajo Dam and Lake from 1958-1962 forced the D&RG to relocate tracks around the lake as shown on the map. (*From a map at the historic display at the Arboles water tank*)

The relocation of the D&RG tracks around Navajo Lake paralleled the relocated County Road 500 seen at the right in this 2021 photograph by the author.

On May 29, 1967, D&RG locomotives nos. 473 and 478 crossed the new bridge over the Piedra River at the northeast end of Navajo Lake pulling twenty empty passenger cars from Alamosa to Durango. The cars were bound for use on the Durango–Silverton train. (*Photograph by Ernie Robart, Friends, Robart Collection, ERNG19670529-0509*)

The D&RG bridge over the Piedra River still stands, and has been converted to a pedestrian bridge at the Watchable Wildlife Area at Navajo Lake State Park.

At the water tank, there is an historic display sign and two D&RG gondola cars in deteriorating condition. Look closely at the side of the water tank, and you can see very faintly the lettering "Rio Grande."

Returning to CO151 heading west, you will arrive at the village of Allison in 7 miles. The D&RG depot was located in the intersection of what is now County Road 329 and CO151. Allison was named after Allison Stocker, a government surveyor in this area of La Plata County. Along with the depot, Allison had a siding for sixteen cars. A post office served Allison from 1904–1954. The Engler family (Francis and Estella) came to Allison in 1904 to settle 160 acres.

> Francis and son, Paris, rode the train to Allison to locate a homestead. They camped in a tent until the remainder of their things arrived on the train two weeks later. All they brought to start the farm was a mare and a gelding, a cow and a heifer and two hives of bees. Their mare immediately ran off with a herd of wild horses. After days of chasing and a lot of help from neighbors, they cornered them in a box canyon and got a rope on her … The train was a good way to travel but there were problems in wet weather. Since the tracks had no ballast, they would sag in wet ground. The train was off the tracks many times between Allison and Tiffany.[16]

Tiffany is 4 miles west of Allison. The D&RG railroad grade roughly parallels CO151 until the grade takes a turn to the south. Continue driving on CO151 to the intersection with County Road 328, and then turn left (south). Turn right on County Road 321 to reach Tiffany. Tiffany was named after Ed Tiffany, a pioneer settler and civil engineer. Tiffany had a post office from 1907–1954, and a D&RG siding accommodating thirty-three cars. Besides cattle and sheep, farmers in the area raised oats, wheat, and hay, shipping out their products on the D&RG to Durango or Denver. Some livestock went on to the stockyards in Kansas City. An early pioneer family in Tiffany was the John E. Carlson family:

> In 1906, when young John was 10, his father heard about land opening for settlement in Southwest Colorado. John E. Carlson bought the land under the Desert Land Application. He bought a place near Tiffany and moved the family. The trip took four days by train [from Denver]. The family moved their possessions in five boxcars. This included two dogs, two horses, two cows and some chickens, plus a rake and a mowing machine … Life was hard at Tiffany, there wasn't a bridge, a fence or a house in sight except for the railroad section foreman's house. Otherwise, it was just sagebrush.[17]

The most prominent building still standing in Tiffany today is the Iglesia de San Antonio Catholic Church built in 1928. In 2019, the deteriorating building was named to the Colorado Most Endangered Places List. This should help the church attract preservation funds.

> [The church] is one of the few remaining original buildings built by Hispanic communities in southern Colorado and northern New Mexico who moved north in

No date was listed for this winter photograph of D&RG no. 482 taking on water at the Arboles tank. (*Unknown photographer, Friends, Dorman Collection, RDS068-026*)

It was a much sunnier and warmer day than in the previous photograph at the Arboles water tank when the author photographed it in May 2021.

D&RG gondola car no. 836 rests on display at the Arboles water tank in May 2021.

Travelers are waiting at the D&RG depot in Allison in the mid-1940s. County Road 329 today is roughly where the tracks and depot were, and the false-front store behind the house at the far right, sits today on Colorado Highway 151. (*Unknown photographer, Friends, Dorman Collection, RD008-013*)

The false-front store in Allison is still there, as seen by the author in May 2021.

the early 20th century to create towns on the then-new route of the Denver and Rio Grande Railroad.[18]

The church still holds one Mass each year on the feast day of St. Anthony, on June 9 at noon. On a visit to the church in 2021, it appeared that no work had yet begun on restoration.

Unfortunately, there is no direct route to follow the D&RG grade from Tiffany 4 miles west to La Boca today. The railroad plunged down Spring Creek Canyon, but the route is blocked by gated private property. If you backtrack to Road 321, follow it north to Road 322, and then circle back south on Road 322 to Colorado Highway 172, you will eventually reach La Boca. This is a very scenic but slow route, and it is difficult to find the road signs. An easier route is to go back to Tiffany and take CO151 to Ignacio, then CO172 south to La Boca. Is it worth the effort to get to La Boca? It certainly is, as there is a wonderful D&RG bridge over Los Pinos River there.

The bridge was built in 1881 as the D&RG continued building toward Durango. After the railroad era, local residents drove automobiles over the bridge to get to Tiffany and Ignacio. Over time, the boards on the surface of the bridge deteriorated and it became unsafe to drive across. In 2020, the Southern Ute Tribe decided to repair the bridge surface. The steel trestle was still in excellent condition.

"Tribal Council instructed us to replace the deck," explained Interim Director of Construction and Project Management, Garry Fulks. "Three different options were

After regular passenger service on the D&RG ceased in 1951, there were occasional chartered passenger excursions such as the "Kiwanis Kolor Karavan," led by engine no. 473, seen here eastbound at Tiffany on October 3, 1965. (*Photograph by Ernie Robart, Friends, Robart Collection, ERNG19651003-0070*)

In 2021, the Iglesia de San Antonio Catholic Church in Tiffany is seen at the lower left with its steeple and metal roof. The snow-capped La Plata Mountains tower to the west.

A close-up view of the church in Tiffany in May 2021, shows deteriorating stucco and cracks on the exterior walls. Fundraising is ongoing for the repair of the church, which was built in 1928.

The siding at Tiffany is shown in this view taken by John W. Barriger III on September 25, 1935. Note the false-front store on the left. It is still standing, as seen in the next photograph. (*Friends, Dorman Collection, RD008-077*)

Tiffany store, which had been used as a residence, is seen in deteriorating condition in May 2021.

discussed, and it was decided to do a slab on deck." This option features a steel deck on the bottom and a slab of concrete on top to make up a new road. This option gives the bridge better integrity to hold vehicles on the bridge while also cutting the expense. "The Southern Ute Indian Tribe felt there was a responsibility of giving an option of access," said Fulks. "The bridge gives access to a cemetery where tribal members are buried, access for oil and gas workers, and access for tribal member recreation."[19]

La Boca means "the mouth" in Spanish and probably refers to the mouth of the canyon where Spring Creek flows into Los Pinos (Pine) River. La Boca had a section house, water tank, and a siding for twenty-eight cars. The original 50,000-gallon water tank was built in 1881 and replaced in 1910. The source of water was originally a well, but after the well failed, the water came from the river. The water tank is gone today, but the bridge remains and is safe to drive across thanks to the new deck completed by the Southern Ute Tribe. Tribal elder Georgia McKinley recalls riding the train as a young girl: "We would ride the train into Ignacio from La Boca for the Tribal Fair or during San Ignacio. We would ride back down [to La Boca] and have to walk home."[20] To view the La Boca bridge today, turn left from CO172 into the area marked as "La Boca Ranch."

Heading back north on CO172, it is about 7 miles to Ignacio, which is the headquarters of the Southern Ute Tribe and today features the Sky Ute Casino and the Southern Ute Museum. Ignacio is named after a famous Ute chief. The Southern Ute Agency was established here in 1877, four years before the arrival of the D&RG. The tribe has approximately 1,400 members today and encompasses 681,000 acres (1,064 square miles). The D&RG had a large station in Ignacio and an extensive siding for sixty-two cars.

On August 25, 1966, D&RG no. 492 is eastbound pulling a freight across the bridge at La Boca over the Pine River. La Boca is just out of view to the right. (*Photograph by Ernie Robart, Friends, Robart Collection, ERNG19660825-0090*)

Double-headed D&RG nos. 473 and 478 cross the La Boca bridge over the Pine River heading west to Durango on May 29, 1967. The engines are pulling twenty empty passenger cars from Alamosa to Durango for use on the Silverton train. (*Photograph by Ernie Robart, Friends, Robart Collection, ERNG19670529-0510*)

The standard 50,000-gallon water tank was built in 1886 and was supplied by a branch of Los Pinos River nearby. Unfortunately, the railroad heritage of Ignacio has disappeared.

> [However] if asked, many elders raised within the La Boca and Ignacio area will remember the distant rumble and whistle of the train pulling into the depots. The Ignacio Depot was established near where the current Southern Ute Utilities Division is located.[21]

As you proceed north on CO172, the Utilities Division is located at the very south entrance of town. There is a large open area where the station was and views there match the old location photographs of the station.

As the D&RG continued its climb up from the low point at La Boca (6,177 feet), through Ignacio (6,437 feet), it reached a flat area 7 miles to the north, which was originally called "Grommet," (elevation 6,611 feet). As the area was settled a post office was established at Grommet in 1904. In 1908, the name of the post office and village was changed to Oxford, because it "sounded better" according to local legend. "The townsite map was recorded November 3, 1909, by the Oxford Land and Townsite Company alongside the D&RG railroad by J.M. Denning."[22] D&RG presence in Oxford was minimal, with a siding for ten cars. Today, Oxford is marked by a highway sign on CO172, a fire station, and dispersed houses. The D&RG grade from Ignacio to Oxford is not paralleled by any road today, so simply drive CO172 between the two towns.

The next stop north for the D&RG was Florida, 5 miles from Oxford. Again, there are no roads paralleling the old railroad grade, so drive CO172 north to County Road 222 and turn right to reach Florida. As you approach Florida you will see the D&RG bridge across the Florida River off to the right (east). *Florida* means "flowery" in Spanish, probably referring to the wildflowers growing along the river. Locals use the Spanish pronunciation (flow-ree-da) for the village and the river. The river flows south to the Animas River at Bondad. The D&RG had a siding for thirty cars at Florida:

> Florida was one of the original water stations along the route to Durango. It had a standard 50,000-gallon tank constructed in 1881. Water came from the Florida River … The tank was located about 650 feet west of the bridge across the Florida River and north of the mainline.[23]

From Florida, the D&RG made a turn south and then back north to Falfa, 4 miles away. Today, you can follow this route along Road 222, which connects the two villages. Falfa was "originally called Alfalfa for the abundance of that crop. In 1904, when the post office was established, it was changed to Falfa, since there was then another Alfalfa in Larimer County."[24]

Falfa had a siding for eleven cars. Just west of Falfa, the D&RG reached its highest point (6,958 feet) since Amargo in New Mexico. In Falfa, Road 222 connects to CO172. You can then proceed north on CO172 for 1 mile to its intersection with U.S. Highway 160. A left turn on U.S. 160 will take you downhill steeply to Durango (elevation 6,520 feet).

A D&RG engine with a caboose trailing, pulls into Ignacio station. Date and photographer are unknown. Note the unusual red and gray paint scheme on the station. (*Friends, Dorman Collection, RDS068-019*)

On May 28, 1966, Ernie Robart photographed a Rocky Mountain Railroad Club excursion train pulling into the Ignacio station. Notice the outline of the mountain behind the train, as the mountain is seen again in the next photograph. (*Friends, Robart Collection, ERNG19660528-0763*)

Left: In 2021, the Ignacio station is long gone, but the distinctive mountain to the south of where the station was is still there.

Below: Photographer Ernie Robart continued to follow the Rocky Mountain Railroad Club excursion train west to Oxford on May 28, 1966. (*Friends, Robart Collection, ERNG19660528-0813*)

At Oxford in May 2021, this westward view shows no sign of the previous D&RG presence here.

D&RG engines nos. 473 and 478 arrive at Florida on May 29, 1967, pulling twenty empty passenger cars west to Durango. Just above the "Florida" sign, the bridge over the Florida River can be seen. (*Photograph by Ernie Robart, Friends, Robart Collection, ERNG19670529-05530*)

Eastbound D&RG no. 476 is leading a nineteen-car freight to the Florida water tank and bridge on November 9, 1967. (*Photograph by Ernie Robart, Friends, Robart Collection, ERNG19671109-0240*)

This is the D&RG Florida River bridge in May 2021. The view is west, as in the previous photograph, but the water tank is long gone.

There is little use trying to track the D&RG grade into Durango at this point, as it has all but been obliterated by the highway, roads, and development. However, in 1888, Ernest Ingersoll described the descent into Durango as he rode west in the San Juan passenger train pulled by a T-12 locomotive:

> Near Carboneria [coal mine above Durango], the track describes two tremendous loops in getting down from the table-lands to the valley, and presently, rounding the mountain spur, reaches the Rio de las Animas, which it parallels into Durango along a cutting through gravel and rock some distance above the bed of the stream.[25]

In 1905, the D&RG built a standard-gauge branch from Durango to Farmington, New Mexico (see Chapter 7). The line split to the south 2 miles from the Durango depot at a point called "Carbon Junction," named after coal mining in the area. Carbon Junction was 8 miles from Falfa and had a twenty-seven-car siding. Carbon Junction today has fallen to Durango's extensive development to its south. There is a Walmart store located there. However, Colorado Highway 3 branches off U.S. 160 here to the right (northeast), and immediately after turning right there is a parking area on the right for the Carbon Junction Trail, a hiking trail named after the old D&RG railroad junction.

D&RG nos. 487 and 483 double-head a sixty-seven-car freight out of Durango heading east at Falfa on July 5, 1967. The La Plata Mountains are in the distance to the west. (*Photograph by Ernie Robart, Friends, Robart Collection, ERNG19670705-0260*)

D&RG nos. 488 and 480 double-head an eastbound freight at Carbon Junction on July 8, 1946. The track on the right goes to Farmington, New Mexico. (*Photograph by Bert H. Ward, Friends, Dorman Collection, RD004-109*)

The San Juan passenger train heads east at Carbon Junction on June 6, 1949. (*Photograph by Robert Richardson, Friends, Dorman Collection, RD038-006*)

6

Durango: Capital of the Narrow-Gauge World

Durango's Centennial Celebration of 1980, commemorating the founding of Durango in 1880 in anticipation of the arrival of the D&RG Railroad in 1881, got off to a rip-roaring start at the La Plata County Fairgrounds on the evening of August 13, 1980. Famous western author and summer resident of Durango, Louis L'Amour, spoke the words thousands of travelers have felt ever since 1881: "When I want to renew my inner, spiritual strength, I come back to Durango."[1]

Situated on the Animas River (formally El Rio de las Animas Perdidas en Purgatorio—the river of lost souls in Purgatory), Durango is blessed with natural beauty in every direction with mountains, mesas, and the broad river valley. There is a spirituality to this beautiful land, which does give comfort to the soul. Durango was also blessed with natural resources such as coal, timber, and precious metals. When Animas City rebuffed the efforts of the D&RG to locate its railroad station there, the D&RG simply moved their plans two miles south along the river, and Durango was founded.

> [Durango was] The pet child of the Denver & Rio Grande Railroad Company, by whom it was laid out in 1880, and fostered with a view of making it the future great metropolis of southwestern Colorado … From the geographical position of Durango and by the influence of the railway company, situated as it is in the center of immense wealth in mines, timber, coal, agriculture and stock raising, it has grown rapidly in importance.[2]

Durango has continued its rapid growth. In the 1970s, when the author lived there, the business district was concentrated near the D&RG depot and spread north along the motel district on Main Avenue. To the south of town, there was a drive-in theatre, little else. Today, the town has expanded along the south valley all the way to the intersection of Highways 160 and 550, nearly 4 miles from the depot. The Durango Mall, Home Depot, and Walmart are but a few of the businesses located there. It has indeed become the "metropolis of southwestern Colorado."

Railroad chroniclers Lucius Beebe and Charles Clegg also recognized the significance of Durango's location:

> So strategically located was Durango that it eventually justified the foresight of the railroad management by becoming the focus of four narrow-gauge railroad operations and the recognized capital of the narrow-gauge world.[3]

The D&RG in Durango was the "capital" for the four narrow-gauge branches eventually extending to the four points of the compass—north to Silverton, south to Farmington, west on the Rio Grande Southern Railroad, and east on the San Juan Extension. Town building was underway in Durango in 1881 in anticipation of the coming railroad.

> Durango anxiously awaited arrival of the railroad with town newspapers reporting the progress of the construction crews each week. Tracks were completed to Durango on July 27, 1881. A huge two-day celebration was held on August 5th and 6th.[4]

Dignitaries from Denver including railroad founder William Jackson Palmer and the governor of Colorado were scheduled to arrive on the train on August 5 for the celebration. However, the *Durango Herald* reported on August 5:

> The unwelcome news received in Durango this morning that the special train of Pullman cars, laden with gentlemen from Denver ... was detained at Navajo by a serious washout and could not reach this city before night.[5]

So, the celebration went ahead on August 5, without the "gentlemen from Denver," but they did arrive in time for the continuation of the celebration on August 6 after repairs had been achieved on the rail line at Navajo, New Mexico.

After the celebration, rail construction continued north to Silverton under the supervision of the D&RG's chief construction engineer Thomas H. Wigglesworth, an appropriate name for a railroad attempting to squirm its way up the mountains and canyons. It was hoped that the train would arrive in Silverton in time for the July 4, 1882, celebration. As the date approached, it became apparent that the rails would not reach Silverton by July 4. The tracks were about three miles short of town on Independence Day. Passenger train excursions brought hundreds of people to Silverton for the celebration, but they had to be taken by horse-drawn carriages for the last few miles to town.

> When did the first engine pull into Silverton? There has been a good deal of discussion as to the exact date, but several reliable references say July 8. This is probably when the first construction train arrived.[6]

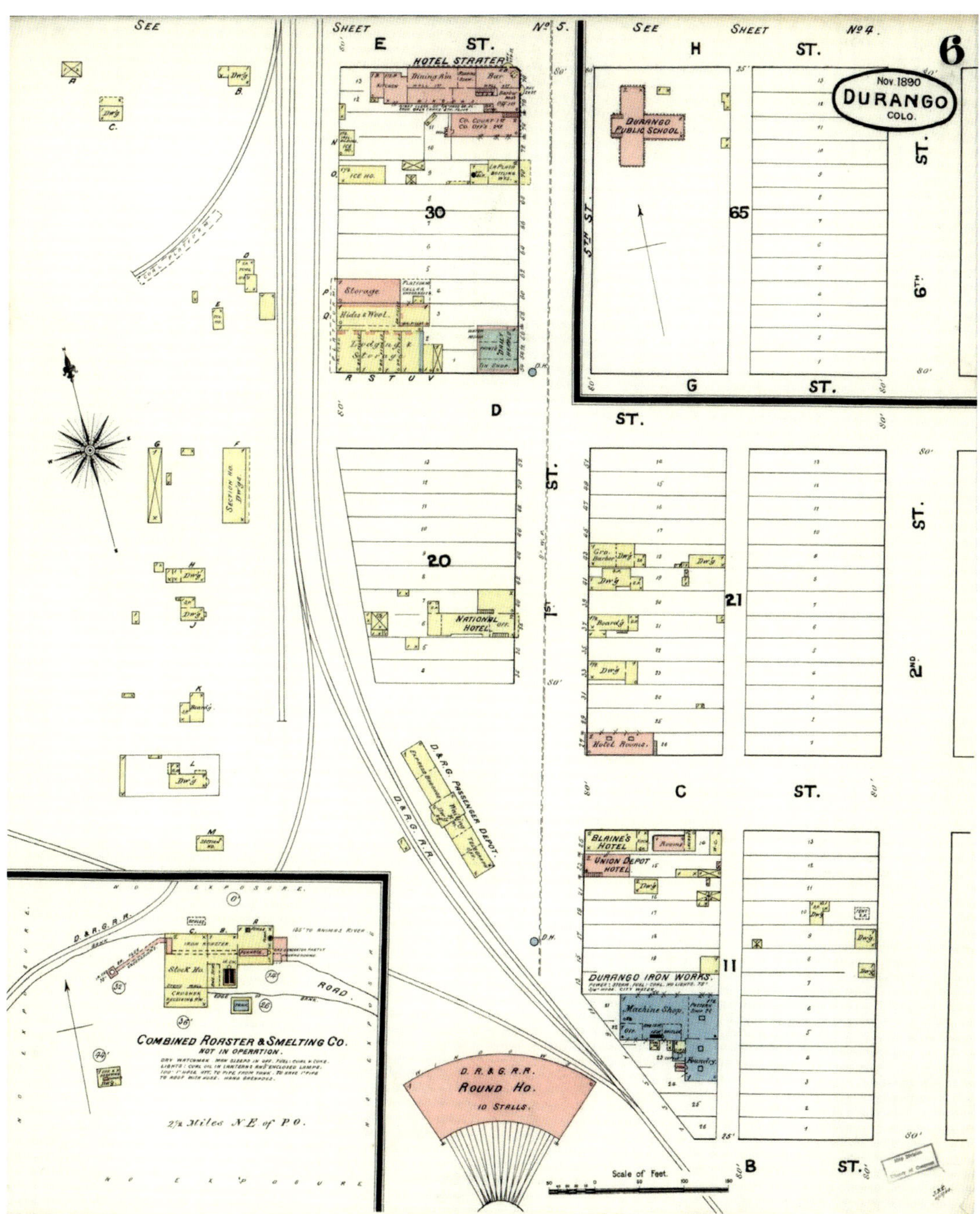

In 1890, just ten years after Durango's founding, the Durango rail yard was fully developed with a roundhouse, passenger depot, and section houses as shown on the map. Two blocks to the north, the Hotel Strater was doing a booming business in its bar and dining room. (*Library of Congress, loc.gov/item/sanborn00987_0031*)

The Rio Grande Southern Railroad was one of the four narrow-gauge branches from Durango. Its railbus Motor No. 2 was parked in Durango in September 1940. (*Photograph by Russell Lee, Library of Congress, LC-USF34-037777-D*)

Meanwhile in Durango, construction was completed on the rail yard facilities. "The D&RG … built an extensive railroad division point with a roundhouse, section house, a pump house, and a standard 24' × 16' 50,000-gallon water tank."[7] The water came from the Animas River. The depot was completed in January 1882.

> [The ten-stall roundhouse] remained essentially the same until June 1965, when the roof and doorways of stalls 4, 5, and 6 (numbered from east to west) were raised so the 480 and 490 series engines could be moved completely inside the building. The rear walls of these stalls were also moved back because these engines are longer than those used in 1881.[8]

Another feature of early Durango was the smelter built across the river from the rail yard in 1881 by the San Juan and New York Mining and Smelting Company.

> The company started in Silverton but moved to Durango to be closer to a coal supply to process the gold, silver, lead, zinc, and copper ores. Between 1948 and 1963, the plant processed uranium and vanadium ores. During the late 1970s and 1980s all traces of the plant and tailings were removed in a massive cleanup effort directed by the Environmental Protection Agency.[9]

The San Juan passenger train is ready to head east out of Durango from the depot on July 2, 1941, led by engine no. 477. (*Photograph by John Maxwell, Friends, Dorman Collection, RDS070-249*)

In the Durango yard in September 1940, engine no. 485 cruises past the coal tower with the water tank to the right of the engine. These structures no longer exist. (*Photograph by Russell Lee, Library of Congress, LC-USF34-037775-D*)

Eight of the ten stalls of the Durango roundhouse, along with the turntable, are shown in this photograph by Russell Lee in September 1940. (*Library of Congress, LC-USF34-037716-D*)

A closeup view of the Durango roundhouse by Russell Lee in September 1940, shows three engines, including from left to right: nos. 459, 375, and 268. (*Library of Congress, LC-USF34-037776-D*)

All that had been left of the smelter was the smokestack that dominated the southern skyline of Durango for many years. Finally, on Tuesday, April 21, 1987, the smokestack was demolished by 50 pounds of dynamite at about 9:40 a.m., "crumbling the foundation and toppling the stack in a cloud of radioactive dust in less than five seconds … to make way for the $15 million uranium mill tailings clean-up project."[10]

Other changes have occurred in the Durango rail yard over the years. The water tank was torn down in 1967, and the coal tower was demolished in April 1968. However, the biggest change was yet to come. On February 10, 1989, fire destroyed the roundhouse. All six operable engines were in the roundhouse at the time. Initially, it was feared that this entire fleet of locomotives had been destroyed. As the wreckage of the roundhouse cooled and was removed, it was discovered that the engines had survived remarkably well. Within a year, all had been repaired and a new fifteen-stall roundhouse was constructed. The new 36,000-sq. foot facility cost $2 million. Eventually, eight of the stalls were converted to a museum by the Durango & Silverton Narrow Gauge Railroad (successor to the D&RG).

The museum incorporates a wall of the original working roundhouse. It houses eight sets of tracks leading to the turntable outside and eight big sets of doors that formerly swung open for the big steam locomotives. Two sets of track have been covered over to provide space for standing displays, while the remaining six are used for the exhibition of historic rolling stock.[11]

A tour of the Durango rail yard in 2021 revealed many ongoing changes. Of course, there was no water tank or coaling tower. Water is supplied to the tenders with a large hose and coal is shoveled in from piles on the ground by a front-end loader. There is still a sand house and car shop. The machine shop was newly constructed in 1989 along with the new roundhouse. Inside the roundhouse, there was a diesel locomotive purchased from the White Pass & Yukon Railroad.

It was being outfitted for narrow-gauge duty to join a fellow diesel already in operation hauling the passenger train to Silverton. Also in the roundhouse were two steam locomotives being converted from coal-burning to oil-burning. Within five years, all the locos will be oil-burning. The tour guide stated that this was done to be more environmentally friendly, as coal burning adds to climate change, and coal was being mined less, so that eventually, they would have no coal supply for the locomotives. New track has been laid at the south end of the yard next to the Wyndham Hotel, and a diesel locomotive engine house will soon be built there.

Things have certainly changed dramatically for the narrow-gauge line since Beebe and Clegg wrote glowingly in 1962:

As late as 1961 the little narrow-gauge Silverton Train running in summer months from Durango to Silverton over the storied route up Animas Canyon continued to be a profitable operation and one of the most celebrated tourist attractions in all the Rocky Mountain region. When narrow-gauge operations everywhere else had disappeared …

Above left: D&SNG engine no. 497 heads toward the Durango roundhouse, with Smelter Mountain in the background on June 25, 1988, in this photograph by the author.

Above right: D&SNG engines nos. 476 and 473 at the turntable and roundhouse in Durango with Perrins Peak in the background on June 25, 1988.

Above left: D&SNG engine no. 473 pulls a late afternoon passenger train into Durango on May 22, 2021. The brick building just above the engine is the machine shop.

Above right: D&SNG open-air passenger car no. 405 rests outside the Durango machine shop and roundhouse on May 22, 2021. The date on the building is 1989, the date of the fire that destroyed the original roundhouse and the date when construction began on this new building.

Engines nos. 482 and 480 are in the Durango roundhouse on May 22, 2021, being converted from coal-burning to oil-burning. The entire fleet of D&SNG engines will be converted to oil-burning within five years.

The Durango roundhouse and turntable on May 22, 2021, show the activity necessary to operate a narrow-gauge railroad in the twenty-first century. To the left is the sand house and tower, then an oil car for the oil-burning locomotives, and to the far right is a front-end loader to shovel coal into the tenders.

The motorized rail car of the D&SNG is covered by a tarp at the south end of the Durango yard on May 22, 2021. Next to it are a passenger coach, oil car, and cattle car.

This new track has recently been laid at the south end of the Durango yard in May 2021. The diesel engine house will soon be built here, right next to the Wyndham Hotel.

the Silverton Train was running filled to capacity and with waiting lines of applicants for space on its decrepit yellow wooden coaches and combines. Per passenger mile in terms of revenue, it was the most profitable railroad operation in the United States.[12]

The D&RG probably would have disagreed with that statement, as their financial losses on the line continued to increase in the 1960s and '70s. The line was put up for sale, and a buyer was finally found in 1981 when Charles Bradshaw, Jr., of Florida, a successful fruit grower, purchased the line for a reported $2.2 million. Bradshaw renamed the railroad the Durango & Silverton Narrow Gauge Railroad (D&SNG) and soon made major improvements to the rolling stock.

Along with the preservation of the railroad's history, Bradshaw wanted a decent rate of return on his investment. More trains were added to the schedule to increase passenger capacity. Passenger numbers on the D&SNG expanded greatly, peaking at around 200,000 annually by the 1990s.[13]

In 1998, Carol and Allen Harper, founders of American Heritage Railways, purchased the D&SNG and have continued its preservation and upgrades.

While today it is wise to secure tickets ahead of time by purchasing them online, in the 1960s it was a bit of a different story as told by *The Railroadians of America*:

Regardless of the means used to reach Durango, it is wise to be at the railroad station at least an hour before the train is due to leave. Be sure to obtain tickets before all are sold, for when the capacity of the train has been reached- about 260- no more tickets are sold. For the modest price of the round-trip ticket, $3.30, one is assured of a unique, incomparable and unforgettable day's outing.[14]

The Railroadians also noted that "The train to yesterday will run again tomorrow." One can only hope that this will always be the case.

While the D&RG continued to operate the Silverton train until it sold it in 1981, the rest of the line from Alamosa to Durango and Farmington was proposed for abandonment in September 1967. Narrow-gauge operations had become extremely unprofitable by that time. Improved highways and trucking spelled doom for the line, as did the cost of transferring freight from standard-gauge train cars to narrow-gauge cars at Alamosa. The Interstate Commerce Commission granted the abandonment on July 30, 1968, and by the end of 1969, the narrow-gauge line was completely abandoned.

There were a few freight train and passenger excursions on the San Juan Extension in the final two years.

The last public passenger train to Durango was a Kiwanis Club Special, which made a roundtrip between Alamosa and Durango in the fall of 1966 ... During 1967 there were only twelve [freight] trains operated between Alamosa and Durango, and during the following summer there were only six ... [they] were accomplished with considerable difficulty, and the one-way trip required three days. Equipment had not been maintained adequately, nor had the roadbed, where weeds had grown so profuse that they caused the engines to slip and stall frequently.[15]

Meanwhile, several railfan groups tried to save the passenger service between Alamosa and Durango.

> Public pressure placed the question of the railroad before state and federal agencies during 1967 and 1968, resulting in a proposal that the National Park Service purchase all or part of the D&RGW narrow-gauge lines, including the Alamosa Shops, and operate or display it as a National Monument. Following a well-publicized inspection trip over the road in November 1968, the Park Service retreated into a series of studies and responses, and eventually dropped the project as too expensive and impractical.[16]

The National Park Service inspection train ran on November 23 and 24, 1968, from Durango to Alamosa. Park Service officials were bussed from the Southwest Regional Office in Santa Fe to Durango to start the trip. The train consisted of engine and tender no. 483, caboose no. 0540, combine no. 212, coach no. 331, and business car "General Palmer." Unfortunately, the inspection trip did not result in the creation of a national monument. This was the final death knell for the narrow-gauge. "On December 9, 1968, the recently overhauled #481 hauling rolling stock needed for the Silverton Branch, made the final trip from Alamosa to Durango."[17] "Left in Durango were the three remaining 470s, the 464, and the 481. All of the other remaining locomotives were brought to Alamosa for storage. The track west of Chama was soon removed."[18]

Though the San Juan Extension of the D&RG was gone, its memory lives on in the praises of Beebe and Clegg:

> Down the years the Denver & Rio Grande Railroad ... has been with the exception of mining itself, the most important single fact in the economy and life of Colorado ... Of all the railroads that have come and gone in Colorado, the Rio Grande with its modest beginning in three-foot gauge has been the most tenacious and abiding ... the Rio Grande was the first of the narrow gauges in the region; it was the pioneer, and this panache of splendor must cleave to its memory forever.[19]

7

The Farmington Branch

Why in the world would the D&RG build a standard-gauge line from Durango to Farmington, New Mexico, in 1905 only twenty-four years after completing the narrow gauge to Durango? The answer is competition. Extensive coal fields lay to the west of Durango near Hesperus. Arizona copper mines had their eyes upon this coal source for smelting their ore. Southern Pacific Railroad president Edward Harriman planned to form the Arizona and Colorado Railroad to access this coal from Farmington. Harriman would build north from Gallup, New Mexico, to Farmington to Hesperus along the La Plata River. The D&RG rushed to build a standard gauge line to Farmington to control the freight traffic, also hoping to join up with the standard gauge Arizona and Colorado Railroad, which would be built to Farmington.

Southern Pacific had surveyors working up and down the valleys to link the coal fields around Durango with Arizona and filed incorporation papers for several lines including the "Arizona and Colorado Railroad Company of New Mexico" in October 1904 … A third rail from Carbon Junction permitted access of the standard gauge rolling stock into the Durango yards, a situation which prevailed for many years … [when] the threat of a rival was removed, the gauge of this branch was changed in 1923 to conform with the neighboring narrow gauge.[1]

Certainly, the Farmington branch had an unusual origin:

[The Farmington branch] was not built with any hope of being a contributor to Rio Grande profits, but as a countermove in a battle of railroad giants … The Farmington branch was like an inflamed appendix and caused about as much misery. Until it was converted to narrow gauge it caused the Rio Grande a lot of pains.[2]

Durango historian Josie Moore Crum likened the Farmington branch to indigestion:

> This was the time that the D&RG swallowed something that gave it indigestion. First it was out the expense of the court battle [with the Southern Pacific] … for eighteen years it had all of the trouble of operating this one piece of standard gauge where everything else was narrow; in 1923 it had the expense of changing to narrow gauge; and lastly … it has had to take all the jeers and insults local inhabitants could invent.[3]

One of the jeers lobbed was that D&RGW stood for "Dangerous and Rapidly Growing Worse," and another was "Dogs and Rats Go West."[4]

What really bothered Farmington residents was the slow and unreliable service on the line. After all, it took three hours to cover the 49 miles from Farmington to Durango. Also, the freight service was completely undependable. It seems that the Durango freight handlers were somewhat nonchalant about their job:

> Durango workers' attitude was that they were seldom behind schedule more than two months. Items shipped from San Juan County [New Mexico] endured quite a journey. They started out on standard gauge until they reached Durango. In Durango, the cargo was removed and placed on a narrow-gauge train. This train went to Alamosa, Colorado. Once at Alamosa, freight was once again transferred to standard gauge for shipment to other destinations. The reverse procedure was the same for freight coming to [Farmington]. Sometimes furniture and belongings arriving by train looked quite used by the time it finally arrived at the end of the line in Farmington.[5]

Finally, in 1923, with the threat of competition from the Southern Pacific removed, the D&RG converted the Farmington branch to narrow gauge.

> Since there seemed to be no prospect of the Farmington branch being extended southward, local residents petitioned the D&RGW asking that the line be changed to narrow gauge to cut down on transfers and speed up the shipping process. This was one of the [few] times that the railroad conceded to a request. The railroad shut down Friday, August 30, 1923. Crews worked all through the weekend to move the standard gauge over to narrow gauge. The first narrow gauge arrived in Farmington on September 3. That fall, San Juan County shipped an estimated 175 to 200 cars of apples.[6]

The apple-growing and shipping activities in San Juan County earned the Farmington train a tongue-in-cheek nickname: the "Red Apple Flyer."

> For many years, the branch subsisted by hauling agricultural products and general freight … Although the Farmington branch had not fulfilled its original purpose as a transportation outlet for coal, the San Juan Basin was also rich in natural gas. After World War II, exploration and development of the natural gas began. Starting in 1952, drilling activities and construction of pipelines to bring the gas to market resulted in daily 70-car trains of supplies.[7]

Most of the pipe for drilling and pipelines was produced at the steel mill in Pueblo, Colorado.

> Drilling operations required substantial amounts of pipe, a bulky commodity from the mills at Pueblo that was destined for remote areas. Shipped by standard gauge over La Veta Pass, the pipe arrived at Alamosa where it was stored and transshipped via narrow gauge. Farmington was to become the busiest agency on the narrow gauge. Additional track was laid there and at Aztec for handling what was to be an immense increase in traffic.[8]

An unforeseen problem developed with the length of the pipe. Most pipe sections were 50 feet long, whereas the narrow-gauge gondola cars were only 31 feet long. To solve the problem, the ends of the gondolas were cut out and an idler flat car was placed between each car of pipe to keep the pipe ends apart.

Agricultural commodities continued to be shipped on the Red Apple Flyer in the 1950s and 1960s, as well as pipe. "1950 saw 28,000 lambs shipped from Farmington by rail. They were valued at $400,000."[9] However, the D&RG halted all passenger service on the line in 1951 when the New Mexico Legislature granted the cessation of that service. There was a particularly severe winter in southern Colorado in 1964–65, and heavy snow blocked the rail line to Farmington. Instead of clearing the tracks of snow, the D&RG applied to the Interstate Commerce Commission to ship the freight from Durango to Farmington by truck on its Rio Grande Motorway. The request was granted, and it was a prelude to the abandonment of the line in 1968. "Five trains totaling 156 cars came to Farmington in 1968. The last trip of the Red Apple Flyer from Durango to Farmington was August 31, 1968."[10]

Tracking the narrow-gauge line from Durango to Farmington today is problematic. Highways and development have covered over most of the roadbed, and few railroad structures remain. Those that do remain, though, are worth the drive south from Durango. As discussed in Chapter 6, Carbon Junction in Durango is no longer in existence. It was here, 2 miles south of the Durango station, that the rails branched off to Farmington. Begin your journey south by turning south to County Road 213 at the Home Depot store on U.S. Highway 160/550. You will immediately cross the bridge over the Animas River and follow along its west bank. However, the railroad followed the east bank of the river after turning south at Carbon Junction. So, as you travel south on Road 213, you will have to gaze across the Animas and imagine the Red Apple Flyer creeping along on the other side of the river. There is no access across private property in this area.

Some 8 miles south of Carbon Junction, the Flyer paused at the Posta siding, which could accommodate thirteen cars. Across the river to the west was the small community of La Posta, which is Spanish for "post" or "stop," referring to the stagecoach stop at La Posta prior to the railroad, where horses were exchanged for fresh steeds. There are a few homes at La Posta today, and the community is marked by the La Posta cemetery on the east side of the road.

Some 5 miles south of La Posta, the Flyer stopped at the Bondad siding where fifteen cars could be located. "*Bondad* is Spanish for 'goodness.' However, a local tradition claims that the site was named after a family called Bonds."[11] In another 2 miles, the

Left: On August 23, 1966, D&RG engine no. 492 was southbound pulling a thirty-six-car freight over the Wilson Gulch trestle, just south of Carbon Junction. In the mid-distance, the Durango drive-in theater screen can be seen. (*Photograph by Ernie Robart, Friends, Robart Collection, ERNG19660823-0080*)

Below: D&RG no. 492 heads a freight north from Farmington to Durango near La Posta, May 27, 1966. La Posta village is seen to the bottom right, with the Animas River above it, and the train across the valley toward the middle of the photograph. (*Photograph by Ernie Robart, friends, Robart Collection, ERNG19660527-1483*)

train stopped at the Bondad water tank along the Animas River. "A standard 24' ×
16' 50,000-gallon tank was constructed in 1905. A 12' × 14' pump house was also
built that same year ... The tank still stands and was for sale all during the 1980s and
1990s."[12] No one seems to have purchased the tank as it was still standing in 2021,
but it looked in desperate condition with collapse a real possibility.

As you travel south on County Road 213, you will eventually come to its junction with
U.S. 550. Turn right (south) on U.S. 550. In about ½ mile, between mile marker 3 and 2, you
will see the Bondad water tank to the left, and in another ¾ mile beyond that, the D&RG
bridge over the Animas River. U.S. 550 is an extremely busy highway, and it is difficult to
stop here for photographs. If traffic allows, it is possible to pull over to the left shoulder for
photos. Actually, a better view of the structures can be seen northbound on U.S. 550, so you
might want to wait until your return trip to Durango for photographs here.

Proceeding south on U.S. 550, it is 9 miles to Cedar Hill, New Mexico. Here, the
D&RG had a siding for nineteen cars and built a bridge across the Animas River.
Cedar Hill had a post office from 1892–1996.

Cedar Hill certainly describes the setting of this inhabited community, but the name
didn't simply evolve from mere description. Sometime between 1887 and 1892, at
a meeting of the local Literacy Society, a new name was selected for the growing
settlement that until then had been known as Cox's Crossing. Members of the Society
wrote names upon slips of paper, and the winning name was drawn from a hat. The
name drawn- Cedar Hill.[13]

Some 4 miles south of Cedar Hill, the D&RG had a siding named Inca, which could
accommodate ten cars. Across the tracks was a community called Rosing, named for
a local resident. Apparently, the D&RG chose the name Inca for its siding having been
influenced by the next town to the south—Aztec.

Some 10 miles south of Cedar Hill and 6 miles south of Inca, the D&RG built a station
at Aztec, which was settled in around 1879. It was named for the nearby Anasazi ruins,
which were mistakenly believed to have been built by Indians related to the Aztecs of
Mexico. The station at Aztec was built soon after 1905 when the Farmington branch was
constructed. It burned down in November 1914 and was not rebuilt until the summer
of 1915. The D&RG abandoned the station in 1968 and sold it to a private party who
remodeled it into a home. The station/home can be seen at 408 N. Rio Grande Avenue.
Aztec was quite a busy station in the 1950s, with many carloads of pipe unloaded here,
bound for the nearby gas and oil fields. The siding had a capacity of twenty-three cars.

To continue following the route of the D&RG, turn right on New Mexico Highway
516 at its junction with U.S. 550 in Aztec. You will take NM516 to Farmington.
Some 6 miles southwest of Aztec, the D&RG had a siding at Flora Vista for sixteen
cars. *Flora Vista* means "flower view" in Spanish, and it was probably named for the
wildflowers growing along the banks of the Animas River here.

Farmington is then 9 miles beyond Flora Vista. Farmington is located at the
confluence of three rivers: the La Plata, the Animas, and the San Juan. This area was
settled in 1879 by farmers and ranchers who could irrigate their lands with water

Above: Northbound D&RG no. 492 is taking on water at the Bondad tank on May 27, 1966. A pump house is seen next to the Animas River. (*Photograph by Ernie Robart, Friends, Robart Collection, ERNG19660527-1533*)

Left: The Bondad water tank was in a serious state of disrepair when the author took this photograph on May 24, 2021.

Southbound D&RG no. 497 pulls a freight across the Animas River on the Bondad bridge on September 25, 1967. (*Photograph by Ernie Robart, Friends, Robart Collection, ERNG19670925-0013*)

The D&RG Bondad bridge as seen by the author on May 24, 2021. A gate on private property prevents closer access to the bridge today.

Farmington-bound D&RG no. 492 pulling a freight, crosses the bridge over the Animas River at Cedar Hill, New Mexico, on August 23, 1966. (*Photograph by Ernie Robart, Friends, Robart Collection, ERNG19660823-0100*)

D&RG no. 497 pulls a freight southbound past the Aztec depot on September 25, 1967. (*Photograph by Ernie Robart, Friends, Robart Collection, ERNG19670925-0103*)

The Aztec depot stands today at 408 N. Rio Grande Avenue, thanks to the renovation efforts of its private owner. It looks like a comfortable home with modern conveniences.

D&RG no. 497 pulls a freight through Flora Vista with thirteen carloads of drilling mud headed for Farmington on September 25, 1967. (*Photograph by Ernie Robart, Friends, Robart Collection, ERNG19670925-0163*)

from the rivers. This was a "farming town," and that soon became the name of the community—Farmington. The D&RG completed standard-gauge track laying to Farmington on September 19, 1905, and regular train service to Durango began soon thereafter. As the endpoint of the branch line, Farmington had a station and a water tank, located on Behrend Street two blocks south of Main Street. A visit to this site in 2021 revealed empty lots and a few small warehouses. The station burned down in 1962 when a gas explosion leveled the building. It was replaced with a small metal building for freight, as passenger service had ended in 1951.

Thus, the story of the Farmington branch line of the D&RG comes to a close. A fitting ending is supplied by train engineer Andy Payne who was the engineer on most of the trains from Durango to Farmington from 1964 to the end.

Trips from Durango to Farmington were often very long because of the switching of box cars and gondolas. It would often take 16 hours to make a turn from Durango to Farmington and back … Payne said different conductors would drag out the trip a little longer. He said his least favorite conductor was Myron "Hotbox" Henry who would drag out the trip so he could get maximum pay. He also was the conductor who spotted the most "hotboxes," or bearings which were overheating so they could get extra pay for the delay (while bearings cooled). Payne said that one engineer was so disgusted with Hotbox, that he pulled a practical joke on him. When he went out to relieve himself in the weeds, the engineer whistled off and left. Henry came running back to the caboose, bib overall straps flapping and his own caboose showing.[14]

D&RG no. 492 arrives in Farmington at noon on May 27, 1966. The view is south on Behrend Avenue, with the metal D&RG freight building next to the train. The water tank can be seen at the extreme left. (*Photograph by Ernie Robart, Friends, Robart Collection, ERNG19660527-0803*)

The Farmington station, water tank and rail yard were photographed by Vernon Axt on May 29, 1947. The station burned down in 1962. (*Friends, Dorman Collection, RD007-018*)

D&RG no. 483 arrives in Farmington on August 11, 1966. The station is gone, replaced by the metal freight building with the sign "D&RGW RR CO Freight Depot." (*Photograph by Ernie Robart, Friends, Robart Collection, ERNG19660811-0010*)

8

The Logging Railroad Branches

As we saw in Chapter 1, building the narrow-gauge railroad from Chama to Durango required thousands of cross ties. Since the area was heavily forested with ponderosa pines as high as 150 feet and 4 feet in diameter, the timber industry developed right along with the railroad. Stands of timber along the rail line were the first to be cut and were rapidly depleted. To continue the supply of cross ties needed, the development of branch railroads farther out into the timber stands was required. Five major branch lines were built out from the Chama–Durango line. While they started out as independent lines, they were often taken over by the D&RG. Though the branch lines had different names, "they were built with D&RG material, used D&RG equipment and were operated by D&RG employees."[1]

The first such branch line built was the Tierra Amarilla Southern Railroad, which extended from Chama south 14.72 miles to Tierra Amarilla. *Tierra Amarilla* is Spanish for "yellow earth," which described the appearance of soil in the area. The Mexican government awarded the Tierra Amarilla Land Grant to Manual Martinez of Abiquiu in 1832. The general purpose of the Spanish and Mexican land grants was to try to keep American settlers out of the area. However, as the Tierra Amarilla Grant consisted of ½ million acres, Martinez soon found it was highly profitable to sell sections of his land to American, as well as Hispanic, settlers. In 1883, a judge's ruling gave complete control and title to the land grant to Thomas B. Catron, a Santa Fe attorney. Subsequently, the D&RG had to purchase rights of way from Catron.

In 1891, E. M. Biggs began cutting timber one mile west of Willow Creek and a sawmill town was set up at Willow Creek. On June 4, 1892, the Biggs Lumber Company was incorporated. In July 1892, the D&RG extended trackage 10 miles south from Chama to Brazos. When the branch was completed to Brazos, the Willow Creek mill and town was moved there. The railroad was organized and chartered as the Tierra Amarilla Southern Railroad.[2] This movement of sawmills and towns was standard practice for the times.

Logging Railroad Branches From D & RG Mainline					
Branch RR Name	Start Point	End Point	Mileage	Dates	Today's Roads
Tierra Amarilla Southern	Chama	Tierra Amarilla	14.72	1892-1902	US64/84, NM573
Rio Grande & Pagosa Springs	Lumberton	Flaugh	22.5	1895-1914*	CR357,359, US84
Rio Grande & Southwestern	Lumberton	El Vado,Gallinas	42	1903-1924&	J8, NM595
Rio Grande, Pagosa & Northern	Gato	Pagosa Springs	30.85	1899-1935	CR700, US160
Pagosa Lumber Co. Railroad	Dulce	John Mills Lake	20	1916-1923^	US64
*abandoned 1914, dissolved 1917					
& tracks removed 1928					
^ end date obscure maybe 1926					

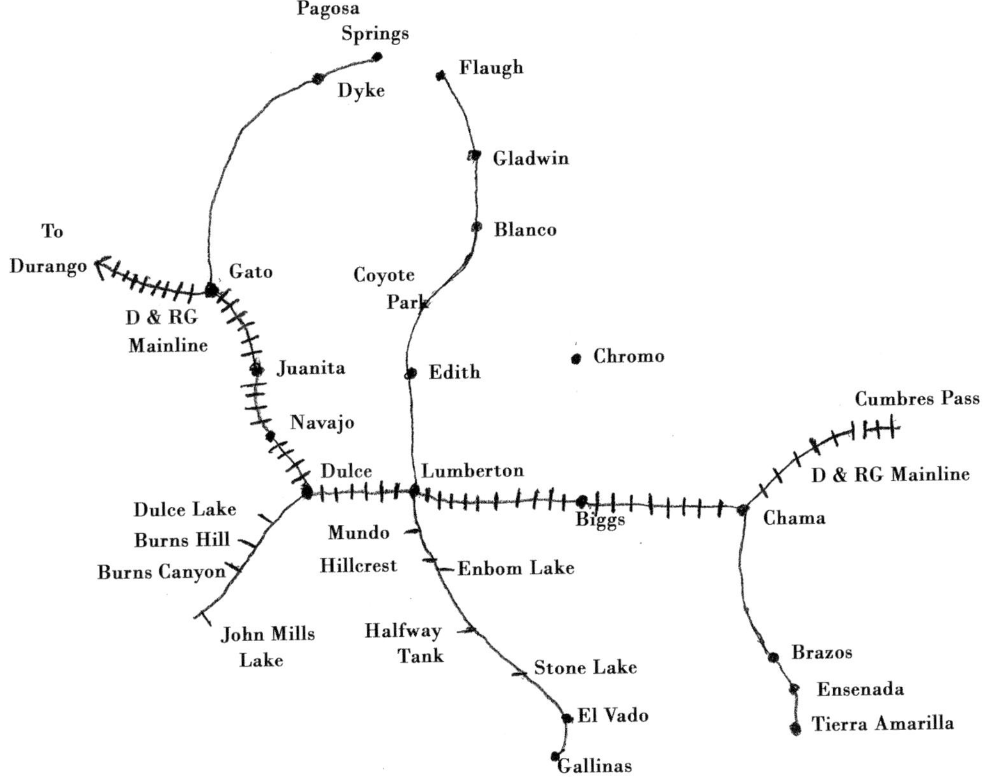

Conceptual Diagram Not To Scale

During the peak 30 years [1890–1920], sawmill "towns" in the timber stands along the Narrow Gauge were built and occupied as long as there was timber to be cut. It was then moved, with the mill to a new location, and took a new name. Branches, spurs and side-tracks ... were built and abandoned as the timber harvest grew and then declined.[3]

By 1892, there were five sawmills operating on the Tierra Amarilla Grant, and they supplied the bulk of the lumber used in construction of booming Colorado towns— Leadville, Pueblo, and Denver. "Oldtimers say the city of Denver was built with timber from Northern New Mexico."[4] Another Colorado boomtown built from northern New Mexico timber was Creede. When silver was discovered in the mountains there in 1891, there was an immediate need for timbers in the mines.

The final impetus for construction of a logging railroad into much more distant stands of timber [south of Chama] was the Creede mining boom which created an insatiable demand for the products of the Chama sawmills ... As early as January 1892, A.T. Sullenberger [of Chama] had sold a million board feet of lumber to Creede customers ... In March, about thirty cars of lumber per day were rolling out over Cumbres, in route to Creede.[5]

As more and more lumber was required in Creede and other towns, the Tierra Amarilla Southern Railroad expanded south from Brazos to cut more timber. In 1896, the railroad built south from Brazos to Ensenada and then to Tierra Amarilla. The Biggs Lumber Company also built a rail spur 10 miles west from Brazos out to Sawmill Mesa.

Tracking the general route of the Tierra Amarilla Southern Railroad today simply requires a drive south on U.S. Highway 84 from Chama to Brazos. Turn left (east) at the sign pointing to Los Brazos, then follow New Mexico Highway 573 from Los Brazos to Ensenada and Tierra Amarilla. Los Brazos was one of the first settlements on the Tierra Amarilla Land Grant. The word *brazos* is Spanish for "arms," referring to the many branches of the Brazos River as it flows west to the Rio Chama.

There are a few homes in Los Brazos today, and its main distinguishing characteristic is the Brazos Cliffs to the east. "These are sheer cliffs of Precambrian quartzite marking the abrupt boundary between the 7,500-foot agricultural lands of the Rio Chama Valley and the 10,000-foot Brazos high country."[6]

Some 2 miles south of Los Brazos is the village of Ensenada. It was settled in about 1864 and may have been named after the Spanish word *encina*, which means "live oak," referring to the many oak trees along the nearby Rio Brazos. Some 2 miles farther south is Tierra Amarilla, which was settled in about 1862. The settlement of Tierra Amarilla grew in importance in 1880 when the county seat of Rio Arriba County was moved by legislative decree from Alcade (north of Española) to Tierra Amarilla.

By 1900, the timber stands south of Chama had begun to play out. Traffic on the Tierra Amarilla Southern Railroad declined. In 1902, the D&RG took over the railroad and ran it until November 20, when they began tearing up the track to be used on the new branch railroad south of Lumberton.

Rising to over 10,000 feet, the Brazos Cliffs dominate the skyline west of the community of Los Brazos.

This view north at Ensenada in late May 2021, shows the snow-capped San Juan Mountains in the far distance.

The Santo Niño Church in Tierra Amarilla was built in 1907, five years after the last trains ran on the Tierra Amarilla Southern Railroad. This adobe Catholic church still stands today.

> The country between Chama and Tierra Amarilla ... once so heavily forested was now stripped of its cover of timber ... Sage and cactus grew. The loggers had succeeded in converting a forest into a desert, dotted here and there with the rotting stumps of once great trees.[7]

Driving through this area today, one can occasionally see a lone ponderosa pine here and there, but primarily, the landscape is open with scattered juniper and piñon pine trees.

> By 1900, most of the large tracts of virgin pine in the "Chama Pineries" had been harvested. Interest turned to the El Vado/Gallinas, Navajo River and Pagosa Springs stands. These tracts were too distant from the narrow gauge to be served by spurs. Because of this, three branch lines were built. Two junctioned with the [D&RG] main at Lumberton and one at Pagosa Junction.[8]

E. M. Biggs of the New Mexico Lumber Company was involved with both the branch railroads from Lumberton. On February 2, 1895, the New Mexico Lumber Company incorporated the Rio Grande and Pagosa Springs Railroad Company. This line would run north from Lumberton to the dense timber stands in southern Colorado, possibly as far north as Pagosa Springs. By the end of July 1895, the tracks had been laid 8 miles north from Lumberton across the Colorado border. The new sawmill town of Edith was established on the banks of the Navajo River. The town was named after E.M. Biggs two-year old daughter, Edith. Yet the question arose—was Edith in Colorado or New Mexico?

Edith eventually proved to be in Colorado, but the uncertainty was such that the town legally fluctuated from state to state, depending on the political affiliations of the administration in the state house in Denver. As Edith [tended to] vote Republican, Republican administrations wanted it in Colorado, while the Colorado Democrats wished it to be in New Mexico.[9]

Ultimately, New Mexico had little say in the matter as it was still a territory, while Colorado had higher legal authority as a state. A new survey of the border revealed that Edith was indeed in Colorado, but the survey also turned up an error in the original survey, which resulted in a tiny jog of the otherwise straight-line border between New Mexico and Colorado.

Although the ultimate goal of the Rio Grande and Pagosa Springs Railroad was to reach north to its namesake town of Pagosa Springs, the railroad decided to build east first instead of north. In 1896, the railroad built 5 miles of track east of Edith to the sawmill at Chromo, Colorado, and built a single-stall engine house at Edith. By the end of 1897, the railroad had built east of Chromo up the Navajo River for 6 miles. Then disaster struck on September 12, 1899, with a fire at Edith, "started probably by a spark from the sawdust burner … the mill and 50,000 feet of sawn timber burned to ashes."[10] This devastation set the railroad back significantly in its plan to build north from Edith to Pagosa Springs. In fact, construction did not begin again until 1901 when 6 miles of track were laid from Edith north to Boone on Coyote Creek.

In the meantime, competition to reach Pagosa Springs arrived in the form of Alexander T. Sullenberger and his Pagosa Lumber Company. Sullenberger and partners incorporated the Rio Grande, Pagosa, and Northern Railroad on April 28, 1899, with the goal of providing rail service between Gato and Pagosa Springs. Track laying began in August 1899, and on October 13, 1900, a construction train entered Pagosa Springs. Thus, the Rio Grande, Pagosa and Northern beat the Rio Grande and Pagosa Springs Railroad to the town of Pagosa Springs.

There was now no urgency for the Rio Grande and Pagosa Springs Railroad to reach Pagosa Springs, and construction northward continued at a leisurely pace as the timber was harvested along the line. In 1902, 7 miles of track were added north from Boone to Blanco on the Rio Blanco. In 1903, 4 miles were added from Blanco to Gladwin. Then, in 1904, 7 miles were added from Gladwin to Flaugh, which became the end of the line, only 5 ½ miles southeast of Pagosa Springs.

In August 1905, another fire struck Edith, and it burned the sawmill and the entire town. The railroad north of Edith had to be shut down, and it was not reopened until the summer of 1906. Stuck at Flaugh, the Rio Grande and Pagosa Springs Railroad had no incentive to continue building northward, as the New Mexico Lumber Company had no land holdings north of there, and the Rio Grande, Pagosa and Northern Railroad had already entered Pagosa Springs in 1900, securing the lucrative mail contract. Disasters continued striking the Rio Grande and Pagosa Springs Railroad as floods in the summer and fall of 1911 destroyed much of the railroad from Gladwin to Flaugh.

Also, on Saturday April 5, 1913, at Edith, "fire destroyed the railroad and lumber company machine shop, the engine house and four locomotives, a loss of $20,000."[11]

Archuleta County Colorado Road 359 begins at the New Mexico border with a bridge crossing the Navajo River. A few scattered homes remain in the community of Edith in May 2021.

This flume still stands in Edith in May 2021. It may have brought water from the Navajo River (off to the right) to the sawmill at Edith.

The Rio Grande and Pagosa Springs Railroad first built east 5 miles from Edith to the sawmill at Chromo, Colorado, prior to heading north from Edith. Drivers today can travel County Road 391 between Edith and Chromo.

That was the final straw as the railroad was then abandoned in the summer of 1914, and formally dissolved on October 24, 1917.

Tracking the general route of the Rio Grande and Pagosa Springs Railroad today involves some back-road travel. From Lumberton, head north on County Road 357 some 8 miles to Edith. Cross over the bridge on the Navajo River and head north on Colorado County Road 359, known as the Coyote Park Road. Continue on the Coyote Park Road until its junction with U.S. Highway 84 where you will turn left (north). In about 5 ½ miles, you will cross the Rio Blanco. Some 4 miles north of there was where Gladwin was located, and 7 miles farther north was the Flaugh Ranch, where the railroad ended. Continue your drive north to Pagosa Springs and enjoy a well-deserved soak in the hot springs.

Biggs and the New Mexico Lumber Company had much more success with their rail line south from Lumberton. In January 1903, Biggs signed a contract with the D&RG "for the joint construction of a railroad which would eventually be absorbed by the D&RG. The new railroad was to be named the Rio Grande and Southwestern Railroad Company."[12] Grading crews began work south of Lumberton in May 1903. The line was envisioned to head south 33 miles to El Vado and then another 9 miles south to Gallinas.

[The D&RG] agreed to furnish narrow gauge locomotives for the use of the RG&SW at a rental charge of $6.50 per day. Furthermore, the D&RG would allow its freight cars to be used on the RG&SW without charge.[13]

Also at Lumberton, the RG&SW built a rail yard that allowed it to interchange with its New Mexico Lumber Company sister line, the Rio Grande and Pagosa Springs Railroad. "From the very beginning the RG&PS and the newly built RG&SW operated as virtually one railroad; engines of the one were used interchangeably on the other."[14]

Heading south from Lumberton, the Rio Grande and Southwestern Railroad entered the Jicarilla Apache Reservation at Milepost 4, after they had purchased rights of way and timber contracts from the Indians. At Milepost 7.36, the railroad built a 1,100-foot straight siding and called it "Mundo," the Spanish word for "world," perhaps thinking they were nearing the top of the world at the Continental Divide.

However, the Continental Divide proved to be another 11 miles south at a spot the railroad called Hillcrest, elevation 7,714 feet. Hillcrest was reached on July 20, 1903. Some 4 miles south of Hillcrest, the railroad built a water tank at Milepost 16, naming it Halfway Tank as it was halfway between Lumberton and El Vado. At Milepost 19, the railroad built a siding called "Lago" which is the Spanish word for "lake," referring to the nearby Boulder Lake (known today as Stone Lake.)

Some 14 more miles were completed to El Vado in 1903, where a sawmill was built on the Rio Chama, commencing operation on April 1, 1904. *El Vado* is Spanish for "the crossing," referring to the shallow crossing of the river there, which allowed horses and wagons to ford the river. An engine house and machine shop were built for the railroad at El Vado. From El Vado, "spurs were built and had hardly been put on a map before the timber served was cut and the spurs torn out to be used on others."[15] Owing to various corporate complications "in 1909, the New Mexico Lumber Company entirely ceased logging south of Lumberton and the RG&SW suspended operations on December 1 that year ... On July 4, 1914, the RG&SW resumed operations."[16]

From about 1914 to 1922, El Vado enjoyed its most prosperous years. The timber industry was booming, particularly during World War I. The New Mexico Lumber Company employed around 200 men in El Vado in 1917. Also in 1917, the RG&SW finished building the line 9 miles farther south to Gallinas Mountain and the village of Gallinas. However, by 1923 the New Mexico Lumber Company ran out of marketable timber in the area, and "in February 1924, the firm commenced moving its El Vado plant and logging operation to a new site near Dolores, Colorado."[17] This spelled the end for the Rio Grande and Southwestern Railroad, though tracks were not pulled up until 1928.

Tracking the route of the RG&SW today requires a start in Dulce rather than in Lumberton, since there is no road south of Lumberton. In Dulce at the intersection of U.S. Highway 64 and Jicarilla Road 8, take J8 south. The road is paved, and in about 7 miles, you will reach Mundo Lake, where the RG&SW had a siding at Mundo. From Mundo Lake continue driving on J8 south for 12 miles to Hillcrest where a road sign identifies the Continental Divide. Just south of Hillcrest, there is a short side road east to Enbom Lake, which the RG&SW passed on its journey south.

Some 4 miles south of Hillcrest, the road makes a series of S-curves, and it was here that the Halfway Tank was located. Some 4 miles beyond that, you will come to Stone Lake where the Jicarilla Apache Nation holds a celebration of its Feast Day every year on September 15. You will notice numerous wood poles set up for arts and crafts booths and food booths here.

Above left: On Jicarilla Road 8, travelers today can see "Lower" Mundo Lake. There is no "upper" Mundo Lake anywhere in sight. The Rio Grande and Southwestern Railroad had a siding at Mundo Lake.

Above right: This is the view north in May 2021, at the Continental Divide on road J8. The Rio Grande and Southwestern Railroad denoted this as "Hillcrest." The side road on the right leads to Enbom Lake.

Below: Enbom Lake offers beautiful views of the San Juan Mountains to the north. Fishing at the lake is restricted to Jicarilla Apache Tribe members.

Above: Stone Lake is a ceremonial ground for the Jicarilla Apache on September 15 each year. The Rio Grande and Southwestern Railroad curved around the lake to descend through the cut in the mesas.

Below: Photographer Ernie Robart found cross ties on the abandoned grade of the Rio Grande and Southwestern Railroad just south of Stone Lake on June 5, 1965. The mesa slope is the same as in the previous photograph. (*Friends, Robart Collection, ERNG19650607-0100*)

From Stone Lake, continue south on J8 until its intersection with New Mexico Highway 595. This route does not follow the RG&SW line, which followed Boulder Creek from Stone Lake to El Vado; however, that is a roadless area today. So, turn left (east) on NM595 and follow it to El Vado Lake. At the north end of El Vado Lake, if you have four-wheel drive, you can turn south on Peninsula Drive and proceed on sand and dirt for just over 2 miles where you will see concrete pilings of an RG&SW water tank off to the left (east). This is where the town of El Vado was located, now under the waters of El Vado Lake. El Vado Dam was constructed on the Rio Chama in 1935, and El Vado Lake State Park was created here in 1962. Peninsula Drive dead-ends at the lake, so retrace your journey back to the north and join New Mexico Highway 95. NM 95 can then be followed along Heron Lake north to its junction with U.S. 64/84 where a left turn (north) will take you back to Chama.

With two branch railroads in operation from Lumberton, lumber barons shifted their interests to the large stands of timber around Pagosa Springs, Colorado. By 1898, A. T. Sullenberger, E. M. Biggs' old lumber rival, had shifted his operations from Chama to Pagosa Springs. He purchased large stands of timber west of Pagosa Springs and with partners formed the Pagosa Lumber Company. In 1899, they incorporated and chartered the Rio Grande, Pagosa and Northern Railroad, with intention to build the line north from Gato on the D&RG mainline to Pagosa Springs. The warm healing waters of Pagosa Springs had long been a camping site for Ute Indians, and the word *pagosa* is a Ute word referring to the sulfurous odor of the springs. The U.S. Army established Fort Lewis at Pagosa Springs in 1878 (later moving it west of Durango) to protect incoming settlers from hostile natives who resented the incursions upon their lands. The town of Pagosa Springs grew up near the fort in about 1883 and was incorporated in 1891. "Pagosa Springs prospered in the 1880s as a stage stop, health spa, center for a sheep and cattle raising region, and headquarters of a small logging industry."[18]

In August 1899, the Rio Grande, Pagosa and Northern Railroad began grading north at Gato, which then subsequently became known as Pagosa Junction. By the end of the year, the railroad laid 14.5 miles of track north along Cat Creek. Grading was also occurring from the other end of the line from Pagosa Springs west to the Dyke Ranch. In 1900, the final 16.3 miles connecting the two segments was completed "by October 13 and a construction train entered Pagosa Springs on that date. Scheduled trains were operating over the line ten days later."[19] The railroad offered four types of service: passenger, freight, mail, and log hauling. By January 31, 1901, the passenger depot was completed in Pagosa Springs, along with a water tank and a one-stall engine house. A schedule was devised so that passengers from Pagosa Springs could depart at 2 p.m. and arrive in Pagosa Junction at 4.20 p.m. in time to catch the westbound D&RG train to Durango. By 1908, the D&RG assumed complete control of the Rio Grande, Pagosa and Northern Railroad. Pagosa Springs residents soon became disenchanted with the service provided by the D&RG as noted by the Pagosa Springs New Era newspaper in 1913:

These concrete pilings held the Rio Grande and Southwestern Railroad water tank at El Vado. The town was submerged under the lake when the El Vado Dam was built on the Rio Chama in 1935.

The El Vado Dam was constructed with steel plates, rather than concrete or earth-fill, to hold back the lake water. There is a one-lane road (New Mexico 112) across the dam.

Construction of the El Vado Dam in 1935 involved trucks and hoists lifting the steel plates in place. (*Photograph from the Heron Lake State Park Visitor Center*)

> The D&RG is still using the dilapidated, combinated [*sic*.], smoking and express car for a passenger coach on the Pagosa Branch ... The branch is probably the best paying one on the system and has the most wretched passenger service. Which is no lie.[20]

Along with passenger service, shipments on the rail line in the 1920s consisted of some lumber, livestock, sheep, wool, and hay. With the onset of the Great Depression in 1929, traffic on the line decreased noticeably. Markets for lumber, cattle and sheep almost disappeared and people could not afford to go to the hot springs in Pagosa. Operating losses for the D&RG on the Pagosa Springs line "averaged $58,875 per year between 1928 and 1932."[21] This foreshadowed the eventual abandonment of the line in 1935. The rails were torn up in 1936. Pagosa Junction became known as Gato once more. Tracking the route of the Rio Grande, Pagosa and Northern Railroad is possible today by driving the "Cat Creek Road" (County Road 700) north from Gato to U.S. Highway 160, and then turning right (east) to Pagosa Springs.

When timber supplies dwindled in the Pagosa area, the Pagosa Lumber Company closed their sawmill in Pagosa Springs in 1916 and moved their operation to Dulce. They began building a railroad line south, with the appropriate name Pagosa Lumber Company Railroad, to harvest the timber in Burns Canyon. This then was the fifth logging branch railroad from the D&RG mainline. Construction went as far as 20 miles southwest into the Jicarilla Apache Reservation, past Dulce Lake, up Burns Hill (elevation 7,715 feet), down to Burns Canyon and out to John Mills Lake. This was very rugged country and the Pagosa Lumber Company "employed teams of horses and a variety of heavy log wagons to move the logs from the cutting site to loading skids along the logging railroad. There another team of horses dragged logs onto the cars using a cable."[22]

By 1923, most of the timber had been harvested and operations declined. The Pagosa Lumber Company seems to have continued sporadic operation until 1926, but the final years from 1923 to 1926 are obscure. "The rail operation was a headache from the beginning, and never profitable."[23]

Tracking the route of the Pagosa Lumber Company Railroad south from Dulce today simply requires a drive south on U.S. Highway 64, which will take you to Burns Hill and Burns Canyon. Approximately 6 miles south of Burns Hill, you can turn left (east) on Jicarilla Road J15 and travel east to Stone Lake, which was on the old Rio Grande and Southwestern Railroad grade. At Stone Lake, you can proceed south to El Vado, or back north on J8 to Dulce. As you enter Dulce on J8, you can see the remains of the old sawdust burner on the right—the last remaining remnant of the large sawmill operation of the Pagosa Lumber Company at Dulce.

The logging branch operations along the D&RG's San Juan Extension lasted from approximately 1892 to 1935 in the various locations. The economic impact on this sparsely settled area was enormous. It spurred the growth of Chama, Pagosa Springs, and Dulce. However, the impact upon the environment was horrendous. The clear cutting of the ponderosa pine trees has left scarred, barren hills and mountainsides for over 100 years now. Traveling through the area today, one can only imagine the grandeur of the great forests that have passed away.

Above left: The Pagosa Lumber Company Railroad passed by Dulce Lake from 1916–1923. Perhaps the lake had more water in it than shown in this dry view from May 2021.

Above right: The Pagosa Lumber Company had a large sawmill operation in Dulce from approximately 1916–1926. This "wigwam" sawdust burner at the south end of town is all that remains.

Endnotes

Introduction

1 Butler, M., *Tracking the Chili Line Railroad to Santa Fe* (Charleston, SC: Fonthill Media and Arcadia Publishing, 2020), p. 12.
2 *Ibid.*
3 Osterwald, D., *Ticket to Toltec: A Mile by Mile Guide for the Cumbres & Toltec Scenic Railroad* (Hugo, CO: Western Guideways, Ltd., tenth printing, 2005), p. 72.
4 www.catalog.archives.gov/id/84125714, p. 2.
5 Butler, *op. cit.*, p. 28.
6 Osterwald, *op. cit.*, p. 68.
7 *Ibid.*, p. 69.

Chapter 1

1 Riskin, M., *The Train Stops Here: New Mexico's Railway Legacy* (Albuquerque: University of New Mexico Press, 2005), p. 115.
2 LeMassena, R., *Rio Grande … to the Pacific!* (Denver, CO: Sundance LTD, 1974), p. 354.
3 *Ibid.*, p. 335.
4 Norwood, J., *Rio Grande Narrow Gauge* (River Forest, IL: Heimburger House, 1983), p. 57.
5 Chappell, G., *Logging Along the Denver & Rio Grande* (Golden, CO: Colorado Railroad Museum, 1971), p. 7.
6 Sumner, D., *Colorado Southwest: The Land … The People … The History* (Denver, CO: Sanborn Souvenir Co., 1973), p. 15.
7 Chappell, *op. cit.*, p. 8.
8 Norwood, *op. cit.*, p. 55.
9 LeMassena, R., 'The San Juan Extension' in *Trails Among the Columbine: A Colorado High Country Anthology* (Denver, CO: Sundance Publications, Ltd., 1987), p. 31.
10 Norwood, *op. cit.*, p. 55.
11 Riskin, *op. cit.*, p. 29.
12 Norwood, *op. cit.*, p 55.
13 Reich, W., *Colorado Railroad Water Tanks: Colorado Rail Annual No. 31* (Golden, CO: Colorado Railroad Museum, 2012), p. 152.
14 Smith, D., *Rocky Mountain Boomtown: A History of Durango* (Albuquerque: University of New Mexico Press, 1980), p. 5.

15 Norwood, *op. cit.*, p. 58.
16 Smith, *op. cit.*, p. 7.

Chapter 2

1 www.catalog.archives.gov/id/84125584.
2 Dorman, R., *Chama/Cumbres with A Little Chili* (Santa Fe, NM: R.D. Publications, 1988), p. 3.
3 Wilson, S. and Glover, V., *The Cumbres & Toltec Scenic Railroad: The Historic Preservation Study* (Albuquerque: University of New Mexico Press, 2001), p. 2.
4 Dorman, *op. cit.*, p. 5.
5 *Ibid.*
6 www.catalog.archives.gov/id/84125714, p. 31.
7 *Ibid.*
8 Osterwald, *Ticket to Toltec*, p. 88.
9 Riskin, *The Train Stops Here*, p. 115.
10 Osterwald, *op. cit.*, p. 75.
11 Osterwald, D., *Beyond the Third Rail: With Monte Ballough and His Camera* (Lakewood, CO: Western Guideways, Ltd., 1994) p. 75.
12 *Ibid.*, p. 69.
13 www.catalog.archives.gov./id/77847435, p. 2.

Chapter 3

1 Richardson, R., *Chasing Trains: The Lifetime Story of the Founder of the Colorado Railroad Museum* (Denver, CO: Sundance Publications, Ltd.,1995), pp. 304–305.
2 Reich, W., *Colorado Railroad Water Tanks*, p. 150.
3 Fugate, F. and R., *Roadside History of New Mexico* (Missoula, MT: Mountain Press Publishing Company, 1989), p. 184.
4 Butler, M., *Images of America: High Road to Taos* (Charleston, SC: Arcadia Publishing, 2016), pp. 30–31.
5 www.tracksacrossborders.com
6 Norwood, *Rio Grande Narrow Gauge*, p. 57.
7 Quoted in Dorman, R., *Durango: Always A Railroad Town* (Santa Fe, NM: R.D. Publications, 1987), p. 135.
8 Chappell, *Logging Along the Denver & Rio Grande*, pp. 30–33.
9 *Ibid.*, p. 33.

Chapter 4

1 www.janofficial.com
2 Osterwald, D., *Cinders & Smoke: A Mile by Mile Guide for the Durango & Silverton Narrow Gauge Railroad* (Lakewood, CO: Western Guideways, Ltd., thirty-first printing, 1998), p. 71.
3 Motter, J., 'Pagosa Junction Loses Noted Landmark,' *Pagosa Springs Sun*, March 27, 2000.
4 *Ibid.*
5 *Ibid.*
6 *Ibid.*
7 www.tracksacrossborders.com

Chapter 5

1 Norwood, *Rio Grande Narrow Gauge*, p. 57.
2 Dorman, *Durango: Always A Railroad Town*, p. 146.

3 Norwood, *op. cit.*, p. 205.

4 *Ibid.*, pp. 205–208.

5 Quoted in Norwood, p. 203.

6 Norwood, p. 208.

7 Richardson, *Chasing Trains*, p. 304.

8 Dorman, *op. cit.*, p. 156.

9 *Ibid.*, p. 169.

10 Linenberger, T., *The Navajo Unit Colorado River Storage Project* (Denver, CO: Bureau of Reclamation History Program, 1998), pp. 13–14. www.usbr.gov/projects/pdg.php?id=86.

11 Arlen, C., 'Journey to The Bottom of Navajo Lake,' *High County News*, August 4, 2003.

12 Hauck, C. and Richardson, R., *'They're Still Building Narrow Gauge in Colorado,'* in Colorado Annual 1964 (Golden, CO: Colorado Railroad Museum, 1964), p. 7.

13 Tharp, P., *The Lost Communities of Navajo Dam Volume 2: Los Pinos, Rosa and Los Arboles* (Aztec, NM: San Juan County Historical Society, 2020), p. 74.

14 *Ibid.*, p. 75.

15 Reich, *Colorado Railroad Water Tanks*, p. 152.

16 Corman, L. (ed.), *A History of Ranching Families in La Plata and Archuleta Counties* (Las Vegas, NV: CreateSpace Publishing, 2021), pp. 8–9.

17 *Ibid.*, p. 59.

18 Armijo, P., 'Tiffany Church Named to Colorado Most Endangered Places List,' *Durango Herald*, February 10, 2019.

19 Martinez, F. 'Ghosts of the Railroad: La Boca Bridge Revitalized,' *The Southern Ute Drum*, November 20, 2020.

20 *Ibid.*

21 *Ibid.*

22 www.tracksacrossborders.com

23 Reich, *op. cit.*, p. 153.

24 Bright, W., *Colorado Place Names* (Boulder, CO: Johnson Books, 1993), p. 52.

25 Quoted in Dorman, *Durango: Always A Railroad Town*, p. 140.

Chapter 6

1 Moore, J., 'Durango Begins Its Centennial,' *Durango Herald*, August 14, 1980.

2 Dorman, *Durango: Always A Railroad Town*, p. 88.

3 Beebe, L. and Clegg, C., *Rio Grande: Mainline of the Rockies* (Berkeley, CA: Howell-North Books, 1962), p. 151.

4 Royem, R., *America's Railroad: The Official Guidebook of the Durango & Silverton Narrow Gauge Railroad* (Durango, CO: Durango & Silverton Narrow Gauge Railroad, 2007), p. 9.

5 Quoted in Osterwald, *Cinders & Smoke*, p. 73.

6 Osterwald, *Ibid.*, p. 83.

7 Reich, *Colorado Railroad Water Tanks*, pp. 153–154.

8 Osterwald, *Cinders & Smoke*, p. 129.

9 *Ibid.*, p. 74.

10 Associated Press, '106 Years of History Zapped in Five Seconds,' *Denver Post*, April 22, 1987.

11 Royem, *op. cit.*, p. 182.

12 Beebe and Clegg, *op. cit.*, p. 199.

13 Royem, *op. cit.*, p. 16.

14 Taber, T. (foreword), *The Train to Yesterday: Durango-Silverton* (Morristown, NJ: Railroadians of America, n.d.), p. 2.

15 Coker, J., 'One More Mountain to Climb,' in *Trails Among the Columbine: A Colorado High Country Anthology* (Denver, CO: Sundance Publications Ltd., 1987), p. 141.

16 Wilson and Glover, *The Cumbres & Toltec Scenic Railroad*, p. 4.

17 Coker, *op. cit.*, pp. 145–147.
18 LeMassena, in *Trails Among the Columbine*, p. 34.
19 Beebe, L. and Clegg, C., *Narrow Gauge in the Rockies* (Berkeley, CA: Howell-North Books, 1958), p. 31.

Chapter 7

1 Myrick, D., *New Mexico's Railroads: A Historical Survey* (Albuquerque: University of New Mexico Press, 1990), pp. 130–131.
2 Norwood, *Rio Grande Narrow Gauge*, p. 90.
3 Crum, J., The D.&R.G. in the San Juan (32-page booklet; no publisher or date listed), p. 9.
4 Davis, C. *A Railroad Here? Meet The Red Apple Flyer!* (Aztec, NM: San Juan County Historical Society, 2005), p. 12.
5 *Ibid.*, p. 16
6 *Ibid.*, pp. 17–18.
7 Hereford, J. and Robart, E., *Rio Grande Narrow Gauge: The Final Years, Alamosa to Chama* (Union City, CA: R/Robb Ltd., 2001), p. 6.
8 Kramer, F., *Twilight on the Narrow Gauge: Rio Grande Scenes of the Fifties* (New York: Quadrant Press, 1976), p. 57.
9 Davis, *op. cit.*, p. 38.
10 *Ibid.*, p. 39.
11 Bright, *Colorado Place Names*, p. 17.
12 Reich, *Colorado Railroad Water Tanks*, p. 156.
13 Julyan, R., *The Place Names of New Mexico* (Albuquerque: University of New Mexico Press, 1998), p. 71.
14 Thomas, J. 'Farmington Branch Grade Good Place to Go Hiking,' *Cortez Journal*, July 18, 2000.

Chapter 8

1 Norwood, *Rio Grande Narrow Gauge*, p. 152.
2 *Ibid.*
3 *Ibid.*, p. 151.
4 Morse, G. 'County Once Was Logging Leader in the State,' *Rio Grande Sun*, August 8, 2013.
5 Chappell, *Logging Along the Denver & Rio Grande*, pp. 16–20.
6 Julyan, *The Place Names of New Mexico*, p. 292.
7 Chappell, *op. cit.*, p. 23.
8 Norwood, *op. cit.*, p. 161.
9 Chappell, *op. cit.*, pp. 41–42.
10 *Ibid.*, p. 41.
11 *Ibid.*, p. 69.
12 *Ibid.*, p. 83.
13 *Ibid.*
14 *Ibid.*, p. 86.
15 Norwood, *op. cit.*, p. 162.
16 Chappell, *op. cit.*, pp. 87–88.
17 *Ibid.*, p. 89.
18 *Ibid.*, p. 27.
19 Wilkins, T., *Colorado Railroads Chronological Development* (Boulder, CO: Pruett Publishing Company, 1974), p. 129.
20 Quoted in Chappell, *op. cit.*, p. 77.
21 *Ibid.*, p. 80.
22 *Ibid.*, p. 105.
23 Norwood, *op. cit.*, p. 161.

Bibliography

Arlen, C., 'Journey to the Bottom of Navajo Lake,' *High Country News* (Paonia, CO: August 4, 2003)

Armijo, P., 'Tiffany Church Named to Colorado Most Endangered Places List,' *The Durango Herald* (Durango, CO: February 10, 2019)

Associated Press, '106 Years of History Zapped in Five Seconds,' *The Denver Post* (Denver, CO: April 22, 1987)

Athearn, R., *The Denver and Rio Grande Western Railroad* (Lincoln: University of Nebraska Press, 1977)

Beebe, L. and Clegg, C., *Narrow Gauge in the Rockies* (Berkeley, CA: Howell-North Books, 1958)

Beebe, L. and Clegg, C., *Rio Grande: Mainline of the Rockies* (Berkeley, CA: Howell-North Books, 1962)

Bright, W., *Colorado Place Names* (Boulder, CO: Johnson Books, 1993)

Butler, M., *Images of America: High Road to Taos* (Charleston, SC: Arcadia Publishing, 2016)

Butler, M., *Tracking the Chili Line Railroad to Santa Fe* (Charleston, SC: Fonthill Media and Arcadia Publishing, 2020)

Catalog.archives.gov/id/84125584

Catalog.archives.gov/id/84125714

Catalog.archives.gov/id/77847435

Chant, C. *The History of North American Steam* (Edison, NJ: Chartwell Books, 2007)

Chappell, G., *Logging Along the Denver & Rio Grande* (Golden, CO: Colorado Railroad Museum, 1971)

Coker, J., 'One More Mountain to Climb' in *Trails Among the Columbine: A Colorado High Country Anthology*, pp. 136-160 (Denver, CO: Sundance Publications Ltd., 1987)

Corman, L. (ed.), *A History of Ranching Families in La Plata and Archuleta Counties* (Las Vegas, NV: CreateSpace Publishing, 2021)

Crum, J., *The D&RG In the San Juan* (no publisher or date listed)

Davis, C., *A Railroad Here? Meet The Red Apple Flyer* (Aztec, NM: San Juan County Historical Society, 2005)

Dorman, R., *Chama/Cumbres with A Little Chili* (Santa Fe, NM: R.D. Publications, 1988)

Dorman, R., *Durango: Always A Railroad Town* (Santa Fe, NM: R.D. Publications, 1987)

Fugate, F. and Fugate, R., *Roadside History of New Mexico* (Missoula, MT: Mountain Press Publishing Company, 1989)

Hereford, J. and Robart, E., *Rio Grande Narrow Gauge: The Final Years, Alamosa to Chama* (Union City, CA: R/Robb Ltd., 2001)

Hauck, C. and Richardson, R., 'They're Still Building Narrow Gauge in Colorado,' in *Colorado Annual 1964*, pp. 7–9 (Golden, CO: Colorado Railroad Museum, 1964)

Janofficial.com

Julyan, R., *The Place Names of New Mexico* (Albuquerque: University of New Mexico Press, 1998)

Kramer, F., *Twilight on the Narrow Gauge: Rio Grande Scenes of the Fifties* (New York: Quadrant Press, 1976)

LeMassena, R., *Rio Grande … to the Pacific!* (Denver, CO: Sundance Publications Ltd., 1974)

LeMassena, R., 'The San Juan Extension,' in *Trails Among the Columbine: A Colorado High Country Anthology*, pp. 18–135 (Denver, CO: Sundance Publications Ltd., 1987)

Linenberger, T., *The Navajo Unit Colorado River Storage Project* (Denver, CO: Bureau of Reclamation History Program, 1998)

Martinez, F., 'Ghosts of the Railroad: La Boca Bridge Revitalized,' *The Southern Ute Drum* (Ignacio, CO: November 20, 2020)

Moore, J., 'Durango Begins Its Centennial,' *The Durango Herald* (Durango, CO: August 14, 1980)

Morse, G., 'County Once Was Logging Leader in the State,' *The Rio Grande Sun* (Española, NM: August 8, 2013)

Motter, J. 'Pagosa Junction Loses Noted Landmark,' *Pagosa Springs Sun* (Pagosa Springs, CO: March 27, 2000)

Myrick, D., *New Mexico's Railroads: A Historical Survey* (Albuquerque: University of New Mexico Press, 1990)

Norwood, J., *Rio Grande Narrow Gauge* (River Forest, IL: Heimburger House, 1983)

Osterwald, D., *Beyond the Third Rail: With Monte Ballough and His Camera* (Lakewood, CO: Western Guideways, Ltd., 1994)

Osterwald, D., *Cinders & Smoke: A Mile by Mile Guide for the Durango & Silverton Narrow Gauge Railroad* (Lakewood, CO: Western Guideways, Ltd., thirty-first printing, 1998)

Osterwald, D., *Ticket to Toltec: A Mile by Mile Guide for the Cumbres & Toltec Scenic Railroad* (Hugo, CO: Western Guideways Ltd., tenth printing, 2005)

Reich, W., *Colorado Railroad Water Tanks: Colorado Rail Annual No. 31* (Golden, CO: Colorado Railroad Museum, 2012)

Richardson, R., *Chasing Trains: The Lifetime Story of the Founder of the Colorado Railroad Museum* (Denver, CO: Sundance Publications Ltd., 1995)

Riskin, M., *The Train Stops Here: New Mexico's Railway Legacy* (Albuquerque: University of New Mexico Press, 2005)

Royem, R., *America's Railroad: The Official Guidebook of the Durango & Silverton Narrow Gauge Railroad* (Durango, CO: Durango & Silverton Narrow Gauge Railroad, 2007)

Smith, D., *Rocky Mountain Boomtown: A History of Durango* (Albuquerque: University of New Mexico Press, 1980)

Sumner, D., *Colorado Southwest: The Land … The People … The History* (Denver, CO: Sanborn Souvenir Co., 1973)

Taber, T. (foreword), *The Train to Yesterday: Durango-Silverton* (Morristown, NJ: Railroadians of America, n.d.)

Tharp, P., *The Lost Communities of Navajo Dam Volume 2: Los Pinos, Rosa and Los Arboles* (Aztec, NM: San Juan County Historical Society, 2020)

Thomas, J., 'Farmington Branch Grade Good Place to Go Hiking,' *Cortez Journal* (Cortez, CO: July 18, 2000)

Tracksacrossborders.com

Wilkins, T., *Colorado Railroads Chronological Development* (Boulder, CO: Pruett Publishing Company, 1974)

Wilson, S. and Glover, V., *The Cumbres & Toltec Railroad: The Historic Preservation Study* (Albuquerque: University of New Mexico Press, 2001)